"*Been in the Struggle* speaks to the .... of becoming antiracist along the Damascus road of spiritual courage. Indeed, Regina Shands Stoltzfus and Tobin Miller Shearer offer us nothing short of an always-in-the-state-of-becoming invitation to dismantle the afflictions of bone-deep racism in churches and the society in which they hope to testify the virtues of faith, hope, justice, and love. And in all this the authors' writing compels us to lift up life-affirming celebrations and rich tapestries of sublime Blackness."

—**JAMES LOGAN**, professor of religion, professor and director of African and African American Studies, and National Endowment for the Humanities Chair in Interdisciplinary Studies at Earlham College

"In a book born from friendship, shared labor, and co-conspiring for their mutual liberation, Regina Shands Stoltzfus and Tobin Miller Shearer invite us to explore the terrain of racism and to discover within it the paths of freedom. Through popular culture, personal stories, and the legacy of ancestors, they invite individuals and institutions to take hold of God's redemptive and holy work of systemic and lasting change."

—**MELISSA FLORER-BIXLER**, pastor of Raleigh Mennonite Church and author of *How to Have an Enemy*

"We need a community of witnesses to hold us, to strengthen us, to bear life with us as we struggle against the injustice that structures our society. This book tells the story of two people who have become friends through their work together in dismantling anti-Black racism. In these pages they share the wisdom they've learned along the way—on how to be present to each other, and truthful, as they name the violences of our world."

—**ISAAC VILLEGAS**, pastor of Chapel Hill Mennonite Fellowship

"Regina Shands Stoltzfus and Tobin Miller Shearer have provided us with a story of relational vulnerability full of opportunities that arise from conflict and transformation, frustration and resilience, fatigue and longevity, in their partnership in the struggle for racial justice. As the title suggests, the authors are not new to the struggle. Their collective years of experience working with religious organizations, providing public presentations, and offering academic antiracism consultations position them to offer rich resources to people looking for more than a program or how-to guide. By introducing us to an antiracist spirituality, they invite us to receive sustenance for the struggle against White supremacy from an array of antiracist educators and activists. *Been in the Struggle* offers a vulnerable, truth-telling account of their deep wisdom for dismantling racism and the intersectional implications for engaging in such work. While many see antiracism work only as academic critique or workplace competency, or even as divisive practice, this book refreshingly recommends that spirituality is a requisite for remaining in the struggle for racial justice. This passionately written book is a must-read for anyone who desires to go beyond simple platitudes about racism and find spiritual nourishment for the struggle."

—**DAVID EVANS**, associate professor of history and intercultural studies and director of cross-cultural programs at Eastern Mennonite Seminary

"This book is for anyone who wants to participate in dismantling racism from a place of love, relationship, and deep faith. Through reflections on their work together over three decades, Stoltzfus and Shearer remind us of the possibility and power of relationship and partnership across racial lines and develop a framework for a robust spirituality that is essential to sustaining this difficult work over the long haul. This work will not be easy, their stories remind us, but it will always be worth it."

—**KEN WYTSMA**, author of *The Myth of Equality*

BEEN
IN THE
STRUGGLE

REGINA SHANDS STOLTZFUS
+ TOBIN MILLER SHEARER

BEEN IN THE STRUGGLE

PURSUING AN ANTIRACIST SPIRITUALITY

HERALD
PRESS

Harrisonburg, Virginia

Herald Press
PO Box 866, Harrisonburg, Virginia 22803
www.HeraldPress.com

Library of Congress Cataloging-in-Publication Data
Names: Stoltzfus, Regina Shands, 1959- author. | Shearer, Tobin Miller,
    1965- author.
Title: Been in the struggle : pursuing an antiracist spirituality / Regina
    Shands Stoltzfus, Tobin Miller Shearer.
Description: Harrisonburg, Virginia : Herald Press, 2021. | Includes
    bibliographical references.
Identifiers: LCCN 2021032562 (print) | LCCN 2021032563 (ebook) | ISBN
    9781513809434 (paperback) | ISBN 9781513809441 (hardcover) | ISBN
    9781513809458 (ebook)
Subjects: LCSH: Race relations--Religious aspects--Christianity. |
    Race--Religious aspects--Christianity. | Anti-racism. | BISAC: RELIGION
    / Christian Living / Social Issues | RELIGION / Religion, Politics &
    State
Classification: LCC BT734.2 .S75 2021 (print) | LCC BT734.2 (ebook) | DDC
    261.8--dc23
LC record available at https://lccn.loc.gov/2021032562
LC ebook record available at https://lccn.loc.gov/2021032563

Study guides are available for many Herald Press titles at www.HeraldPress.com.

BEEN IN THE STRUGGLE
© 2021 by Herald Press, Harrisonburg, Virginia 22803. 800-245-7894.
    All rights reserved.
Library of Congress Control Number: 2021032562
International Standard Book Number: 978-1-5138-0943-4 (paperback);
    978-1-5138-0944-1 (hardcover); 978-1-5138-0945-8 (ebook)
Printed in United States of America

All rights reserved. This publication may not be reproduced, stored in a retrieval
system, or transmitted in whole or in part, in any form, by any means, electronic,
mechanical, photocopying, recording or otherwise without prior permission of
the copyright owners.

Unless otherwise noted, Scripture text is quoted, with permission, from the
New Revised Standard Version, © 1989, Division of Christian Education of the
National Council of Churches of Christ in the United States of America.

25 24 23 22 21   10 9 8 7 6 5 4 3 2 1

For my ancestors and elders,
my children and their children—
my work is always for you.
Regina

To Dylan and Zach because you make my heart glad.
Tobin

Contents

Foreword

If we are going to do antiracism and racial justice work for the long haul, we'll need a community of faithful co-conspirators and elders to walk with and learn from on our journey. It has been a shock to see how many new people have begun speaking, writing, and organizing against white supremacy and all its various systemic dimensions since the Black Lives Matter movement first emerged, and even more in the wake of the Trump administration. As someone who had the seed planted for this work in my undergrad years (2000–2004) and since 2005 has been involved in addressing racism in the church and broader society as a significant part of my vocation, I'm grateful for a growing chorus of voices that have popped up in the last few years. For too long those committed to the faithful healing of our racial wounds and transforming our systems and mangled power dynamics have done so while feeling like voices crying out in the wilderness.

While I'm grateful for the new voices that have emerged in recent years in response to our current moment, I'm also grateful for the elders who have paved the way. I have been at this since the turn of the twenty-first century, and I often feel that I don't have the same fresh energy that some of my peers do (which is needed right now), yet I also realize that I have inherited so much from elders who have been doing the work for a much longer time. And there is so much wisdom readily available to sustain us in this struggle.

Unfortunately, our society has not always valued intergenerational sharing of wisdom. However, growing up in a Black church, I would always hear about passing the baton intergenerationally, standing on the shoulders of those who came before, looking back so we can move forward, and what it meant to be a part of the Joshua generation that could enter the promised land only by continuing what the Moses (and Miriam) generation began. Basically, I was oriented to seek out, draw from, and build on the wisdom of elders. Of course, being an elder isn't first and foremost about being old. There are many older people whom I do not see as elders. The way I understand it, elders are those who have more wisdom to offer their community thanks to their attentiveness to their expansive lived experience as well as their own process of creatively and dynamically listening to and inheriting from their own elders.

My anti-oppression journey cannot be separated from my discipleship to Jesus and the communities and traditions that have informed my understanding of my vocation. I was raised in a nondenominational Black church for the first eighteen years of my life. During college I was introduced to Anabaptism and would serve as a pastor of youth and young adult ministries at a multiracial Anabaptist congregation in the city of Harrisburg immediately after I graduated. But it was not until I moved back to Philly to start seminary and was serving as an associate pastor at my home church that I began identifying Anabaptism as an important part of my Christian identity and understanding. I was reading Black theology and Anabaptist theology and putting them into a creative conversation. And there in Philly I met Black, Latinx, Asian, and white Anabaptists (especially Mennonites) who were contextually embodying their Anabaptism in multifaceted ways that broke all my stereotypes of who Anabaptists were. Through social media and blogging I was becoming known for my "AnaBlacktivism": Black theology, Anabaptism, and activism. This would eventually gesture me toward researching Black theology and Anabaptism together, and all the intersections I could find, during my PhD studies. Very quickly, my world and networks expanded. Far from a voice crying out in the wilderness, I discovered a great cloud of witnesses at this intersection. And just a little before that happened, I had also begun engaging in antiracism work among Mennonites across the country. Before I knew it, my research and relationships would begin to overlap in deep ways.

Anyone who has engaged in dismantling racism in Mennonite spaces in the United States for an extended time already knows Regina and Tobin, as well as the assortment of individuals they mention throughout the book, like Calenthia Dowdy, Felipe Hinojosa, Glen Guyton, Michelle Armster, Iris de León-Hartshorn, and many others. What lies behind this book is a community of faithfulness that has shaped me. While I am not Mennonite, I often say I am a friend of the Mennonites, and so much of that has to do with those at the edges of this church movement who have provided me with vibrant community and wise elders.

While I have spent some time together with Regina and Tobin in the same space, I have mostly interacted with them separately. I believe I first encountered Regina through some of her writing on Lee Heights Church and the antiracist witness she inherited within this interracial Mennonite community. We would soon cross paths in various spaces, including Regina's overseeing my invitation to visit and deliver an MLK lecture at Goshen College in 2016. I was privileged to watch Goshen College honor her with a distinguished award for the local justice work she had been involved in. I also met Tobin through his writing before I met him in person. He had written important historical scholarship on Mennonites and race during the civil rights era that helped me fill in some knowledge gaps and provided me with an honest look at what this tradition had (and had not) embodied on the ground. It also provided me my first in-depth look into the life of Vincent Harding, a Black leader who spent a decade in the Mennonite church before departing, though he is more known for his involvement in the civil rights movement, his friendship with Dr. King, and his scholarship and teaching. Tobin and I would connect around these common interests. While sitting with him over meals, I first learned about the decades of work he and Regina had done together and the backlash they endured in those years, which is among the topics discussed in this book. Given that about a third of my invitations to come and do antiracism work have been in Anabaptist circles, I have been deeply aware of how much Regina and Tobin, and so many others, have helped paved the way for my AnaBlacktivism.

This book offers a much-needed prophetic and pastoral word from elders in the antiracist struggle. As you read you can tell that it draws on decades of experience and insight. It is a book for those who have not only awakened to the persistence of white supremacy in our systems, but who are committed to and looking to persevere in this work when it is no longer trendy. The transformative spirituality, deep analysis, and overflowing wisdom in this resource offer quite a contrast to the half-baked hot takes that too often dominate the attention of folks just entering the work of antiracism. In this resource, we are gifted with a faithfulness that understands our interlocking systems of oppression, that exposes cosmic forces embedded in structural injustice, and that invites us to pray with our feet. We need to hear from a lot of different voices right now, but we need this book because we desperately need to sit with our elders and hear from people who have been in the struggle and are willing to pass their wisdom onto us. Regina and Tobin are trustworthy guides, not just for Anabaptists but for anyone committed to following Jesus faithfully in a world organized around white supremacy.

—Drew G. I. Hart
assistant professor of theology at Messiah
University and author of *Who Will Be a
Witness? Igniting Activism for God's Justice,
Love, and Deliverance*

Acknowledgments

Writing a book is always a collective effort. That has been particularly true in this case. We could not have conceived, written, edited, proofed, and saw this book through publication in the space of eleven months if not for the support of an excellent team.

We both want to thank our partners and families for encouraging us and believing we had it in us to write this book. Thank you Cheryl, Dylan, Zach, Terri, Matt, Dan, Rachel, and Josh.

The editorial team at MennoMedia has also been incredibly supportive. Special thanks go to publisher Amy Gingerich for inviting us to write this book in the first place, to managing editor Meghan Florian for being absolutely on top of her game, to editor Elisabeth Ivey for helping us think through the arc and structure of our text, and to copyeditor Sara Versluis for incredible attention to detail (and for catching more than one citational error).

We also want to acknowledge and offer gratitude for our employing institutions—Goshen College and the University of Montana. They provided a stable financial base while we wrote this book and excellent students with whom to explore and test out the ideas about which we have written.

And, we finally want to celebrate and express deep gratitude for the antiracist community with whom we have partnered over the years. The support of and conversations with Nekeisha Alayna Alexis, Michelle Armster, Phil Brubaker, Rick Derksen, Calenthia Dowdy, Harley and Sue Eagle, Iris de León-Hartshorn, Felipe Hinojosa, Alex Kim, Erica Littlewolf, James Logan, Liz Song Mandell, Conrad Moore, Murray Pierce, Jeannie Romero Talbert, Lorraine Stutzman Amstutz, and so many others has been sustained, rich, and lifegiving. Thanks and thanks again to you all.

Introduction

Spirituality is a relational word. As such, it is perhaps coun- terintuitive to begin a book that is critical of much of the White community's fixation on interpersonal definitions of racism with a relational frame.

But strict notions of common sense have never confined most spiritual traditions.

And so we start exactly where it makes the least and also the most sense to do so—by reflecting on our relationship.

For nearly three decades we have worked together in a joint project of dismantling racism. Over the years, we have phased in and out of more intense periods and others more fallow. But our collaboration has been consistent, sustained, and marked by a deep and unremitting foundation of mutual respect. We have also weathered both physical and emotional challenges, geographical dislocation, relational disruption, and simple human failing. Through all of that, we have continued to stay connected and pursued a common goal.

All stories begin somewhere. Ours began in New York City. In the spring of 1993, we had both begun working for the peace and justice division of a religious nonprofit, Mennonite Central Committee (MCC) U.S. We joined our new colleagues at a conference and participated together in a workshop there. During a break between sessions, we chatted about the new "racism awareness" project that MCC had embarked on. Tobin remembers feeling relieved to have found someone with whom he could talk about all the challenges involved in what had originally been conceived of as a two-year, close-ended project. Regina recalls being a bit amused and somewhat suspicious of the motives of this all too earnest and very young White guy talking about racism as if he knew what it was.

Within a matter of months, we had decided to collaborate to plan and host a new conference slated for March 1995 focused on racism for members of our denomination (Mennonite Church) and other groups under the Anabaptist umbrella—those inheritors of the sixteenth-century Radical Reformation movement who went on to organize themselves as Amish, Brethren in Christ, Church of the Brethren, and Mennonites. We each found the work to be lonely and tiring and longed for conversation partners. We would call the conference Restoring Our Sight.

We hoped for 50 people to attend. More than 250 showed up. The conversations in the course of the gathering were intense, widely divergent in terms of levels of sophistication and nuance, and robust.

Really robust.

It had been some twenty years since Anabaptists had attended to issues of racism in any focused, collective way. People had a lot to say.

Something new was emerging, about to be birthed. The image felt particularly apt at the time, as Regina was pregnant with her son Joshua. We anticipated the entry of a new life as we worked together to bring about a new movement. Almost immediately we laid plans for organizing institutionally based antiracism teams and began collaborating with Crossroads Ministry to do so. This Chicago-based antiracism training group equipped denominations to train educating and organizing groups for the long-term work of dismantling racism. Some of their staff had Mennonite connections. It seemed like a natural fit.

DAMASCUS ROAD COMES TO LIFE

In a pre-Zoom era, we communicated regularly by phone and email but less often in person. One of the realities of our working relationship is that we have never lived closer than two and a half hours driving time. Most often, we met in person for the antiracism trainings that we were increasingly asked to lead. In the immediate aftermath of the Restoring Our Sight conference in Chicago, we scheduled a meeting for partnering institutions to plot out what the next steps would be.

Although successful in drawing together a group of nine institutions that would take part in the inaugural offering of what would come to be called the Damascus Road antiracism process, that meeting also revealed several tensions that would persist throughout our partnership with Crossroads Ministry. Two dynamics in particular proved troublesome. The first was that the director of Crossroads at the time, a charismatic and powerful White antiracism educator and organizer, dominated the meeting. Although both of us were grateful for the expertise, longtime experience, and effective record that Crossroads brought to the table, both of us also felt uneasy about how quickly Crossroads had taken control of our emerging process. While we talked with each other about that uneasiness, we didn't know what our alternative might be. We were also very new to the work and couldn't imagine a way forward that didn't include this relationship with more seasoned trainers and organizers.

The second tension was an economic one. Although we shared the title as co-coordinators and founders of the Damascus Road program, the financial arrangement was inherently unequal. Regina already had a full plate, as she not only worked part-time for MCC's Peace and Justice Ministries but also served as associate pastor at her congregation in Cleveland, Lee Heights Community Church. Additionally, she was preparing to pursue a master's degree. The work she did with Tobin for Damascus Road was uncompensated. By contrast, Tobin worked full-time for MCC's Racism Awareness Project and received compensation for doing so. Regina was offering her time outside of her job responsibilities; Tobin's job description called for him to do the work in which he was engaged. As we have reflected on this tension, we both recognize that this is an example of antiracism work unfolding from raced and gendered bodies. Women—and People of Color—have consistently been expected to perform unpaid labor in the antiracism field and elsewhere. While Tobin did push MCC to ensure that Regina and the rest of the training team were paid for doing trainings, he did not push in the same way to ensure that Regina was compensated for the time she invested in co-coordination. Regina recognizes that at the time she bought into that assumption and did not push back either.

Amid these strains, the Damascus Road program blossomed. We assembled a multiracial cohort of co-trainers and, between 1995 and 2000, conducted hundreds of antiracism trainings for Anabaptist groups across the country. Whenever we could lead those trainings together, we did so, particularly at national venues. It was an exhausting and intense time.

At one point, we co-led a two-hour session about racism for several thousand Mennonite youth gathered for a national assembly. Although we had long held and promoted a principle of People of Color having veto power in our antiracism work, the behind-the-scenes preparation process involved one of the first times that we had called upon that principle in our working relationship. Tobin wanted to use a PowerPoint slide of a historical "race chart" illustrating the way the racial hierarchies were taught. The slide showed an orangutan as the next step below a Black person. Regina vetoed that image because she was concerned that displaying it would open the floodgates for racist comments from the White high school–age youth in attendance, and cause potential embarrassment for Black youth. Tobin felt disgruntled by the decision and did not take it gracefully. In any case, we completed the session only to hear one of the moderators exclaim in public session the following day, "That session was just so looooong!"

Despite such setbacks, more and more teams joined. As they did, the training environments increased in intensity. At the second of our two-part training sequence held at a beautiful retreat center in the redwood forests of California, the training essentially collapsed. Attendees at these trainings were teams of colleagues sent by their respective organizations. As usual when working with Christian groups, we began each morning with a short worship service planned and led by one of the teams. Teams were encouraged to draw upon their respective cultural heritages, and they did. One group objected to another group's use of drums and the burning of sage in their worship service, contending that it evoked evil spirits. Later, another group challenged the very basis of the training itself and called out Crossroads leadership for treating the participants like children.

The two of us met to decide how to proceed. And although Crossroads staff wanted to eject the team that seemed to be at the root of much of the controversy, we claimed the authority to make the decision ourselves and closed the event with a long session of silent meditation during which several individuals stormed out of the room and never again participated in our program. We later learned that the training itself had been sabotaged before we even began by at least one person in a conference leadership position who resented being sent to an antiracism training (because it implied racism existed, and this person disagreed with that notion). These kinds of behaviors were by no means limited to this particular training; over the years we have learned that resistance to antiracism work is fairly predictable.

CONTROVERSIES AND CELEBRATIONS

These kinds of controversies—for there had been many others—actually served to strengthen our relationship. We had weathered a churchwide flap over a moratorium we had proposed on short-term service projects. Together, we passed through accusations internal to Mennonite Central Committee that Tobin was psychologically unbalanced and in need of mental health resources because of how he worked at dismantling racism. And we survived repeated attempts on the part of an upper-level MCC administrator to defund, dismantle, and cancel Damascus Road. Others had disparaged the writing we had done about our choice of the term *antiracism*, accused both of us of trying to destroy fragile Mennonite institutions, and disinvited us from speaking at a conference for Mennonite educators after we made public comments about the racist roots of private religious primary and secondary schools.

Still, it was not all controversy and crisis. Regina's congregation in Cleveland had not only called her into ministry there but had also supported her pastoral licensing, an important step in the ministerial credentialing process among Mennonites. The weekend of her licensing coincided with MCC regional meetings held at Regina's church, so Tobin not only got to be present to support the celebration of Regina's licensure but was able to share a few words on behalf of MCC. In his comments to the congregation, he emphasized the grace, good humor, wisdom, and grounding that were already evident in Regina's life and witness.

We continued to offer trainings and support the teams we had helped organize. The Damascus Road antiracism process had become well known in church leadership circles and had begun to reach broader audiences across the church community. We had even opened up conversations with the Brethren Mennonite Council (BMC) for gay and lesbian interests about their participation in the process.

Then at an antiracism training event in the Lincoln Park area of Chicago, leaders of the Black ministerial association of the Mennonite Church informed us that they would withdraw from the process and oppose it going forward if we continued to make connections between racism and homophobia and heterosexism in our training materials. After announcing a break, the two of us went across the street to a restaurant, found a booth, and sat down. We didn't say much of anything for quite some time.

Finally we asked each other what we were thinking. Regina was the first to articulate what we soon realized was the choice that had, at that time, the most integrity for both of us.

Knowing the demands that carrying out that decision would entail, Tobin remembers having to fight against a strong urge to walk out of the restaurant, head toward Lake Michigan, and walk along the shore until he was as far away from the training as possible. We decided that we needed to return to the training space and tell the participants that our personal positions were that there were direct and undeniable linkages in the way the church had exercised racism and how it treated members of the LGBTQ community. We also decided that we would shift from making direct connections between racism and heterosexism in our training materials to inviting each team to make those connections for themselves. The call to BMC the following week was as painful as it was disappointing. We did not work with them again; however, some years later, Regina went on to become a BMC board member and served as board president for a term.

During this time, our relationship with Crossroads Ministry had also begun to unravel. In addition to feeling that we were never really in control of the process that we led, we began to note a set of behaviors in our relationships with Crossroads that left us more than unsettled. At nearly every training, the Crossroads director would at some point lash out at Regina, often claiming that she had not been as forceful or direct or committed to the cause as he thought that she should be.

And so in yet another moment of high drama and crisis, we backed out at the last minute from a national gathering of denominational groups affiliated with Crossroads because we could no longer countenance being part of an organization that at root seemed far more interested in controlling our work than in nurturing who and what we could become.

By 2000 we had officially left our working relationship with Crossroads—despite a reconciliation meeting of sorts held in a Cleveland airport meeting room—and developed a training model of our own that was, to be certain, a result of the years we had spent partnering with Crossroads. This, too, had required an investment of time, energy, and creativity that we and our training partners had only begun to recognize as incredibly energizing and simultaneously debilitating. Despite the revitalization we saw in our work as a result of leaving the Crossroads partnership, we both began to notice that we were feeling depleted by the conflict and its resolution.

STEPPING DOWN

In the aftermath of that decision, our time spent co-coordinating the Damascus Road process soon came to an end. The decisions we came to individually to step down from our respective leadership roles did not directly result from the choice to be less overt about LGBTQ issues in our training materials, but neither were they entirely disconnected. Regina's sense of call to step down was far less drama-filled than Tobin's. She simply knew her time leading Damascus Road had come to an end. The travel exacted a toll on her family, even with a supportive spouse. Being pulled in so many directions—home, church, school—left little room for the energy it took to co-direct a program.

Tobin picked up a berserk intestinal virus after eating a sandwich left in the back window of a rental car while traveling through Southern California on vacation with his sons. Toward the end of the eleven days he spent flat on his back recovering, he realized that he needed to step down, without knowing that Regina had discerned that about herself during the same time period. In retrospect, these discernments felt like movements of the Spirit, which we had previously recognized in our work.

A few weeks later we attended meetings held at MCC's headquarters in Akron, Pennsylvania. We both remember the moment on a sidewalk when we turned to each other and said, "I'm going to be stepping down." At that point, Tobin recalls feeling exhausted, a bit relieved, and filled with a yawning grief. Regina remembers a similar relief, coupled with a bit of guilt. It seemed like the demands of travel, the controversies of our dismantling racism work, and the intensity of years of challenging people to step up and claim an antiracist identity had finally taken its toll. We soon made our decisions public, and in a matter of months, two new directors had been appointed. The organization seemed poised to continue without us serving in the leadership posts.

By leaving those administrative jobs, we were each able to pursue new creative paths while remaining connected to Damascus Road and the organization it in turn became— Roots of Justice (ROJ). For several years, both of us continued to conduct antiracism trainings and attend planning meetings as ROJ left the confines of MCC and, in so doing, embraced a far more intersectional approach in which connections between racism, sexism, classism, and heterosexism were made forthright and uncompromising. About ten years later, Tobin stepped down from doing active antiracism training with ROJ, as he had begun to feel overwhelmed by the demands of meeting pre-tenure requirements as a professor at the University of Montana. Regina found the time, energy, and psychic space to continue doing trainings while completing her doctoral studies and working as an administrator at Anabaptist Mennonite Biblical Seminary and later teaching at Goshen College.

During that period, we had seen our families grow and develop. Children had gone off to college, started careers, and found their own voices. We had always made a point of having our families hang out together whenever we could. Although distance prevented that from happening as often as we would have liked, we continued to stay in touch, and conducted several speaking engagements together and wrote articles that built on and referenced each other's work. Whenever we did connect directly, as when we collaborated with our good friend and fellow academic and antiracism educator Felipe Hinojosa to organize a gathering of leaders of the Minority Ministries Council, a Black, Indigenous, and Latinx church group active in the late 1960s and early 1970s, our relationship settled in with little to no friction or unfamiliarity. The trust ran deep.

In January 2019, Tobin became embroiled in a controversy that received national attention. Although he had earned a certain measure of statewide notoriety for being the "White guy who taught that Black history," a distinction that led to him being the only academic from Montana included on the White nationalist–supported Professor Watchlist, he came under scrutiny for chairing the University of Montana's Martin Luther King Jr. Day committee after four White young women won an essay contest and their photos were released on social media. Hate mail and harassing phone calls flooded in as the controversy showed up in *USA Today*, *Inside Higher Ed*, and the *Washington Post*, among many other news sources. The verbal and written attacks started to take an emotional toll on Tobin, but a particular moment of grace came through when Regina reposted an op-ed Tobin had written about the events along with the comment, "This is my friend."

At some points people have asked us what has sustained our friendship and working relationship, this long-term connection between a Black professor of peace, justice, and conflict studies whose students adore her so much that they have designed and marketed a "Regina Shands Stoltzfus" mug and a White professor of history and African American studies whose students say they take his classes so that they can score an invitation to the soup and pie nights he hosts each year. Regina says of Tobin,

> I know very few White people whom I trust as much to do this work, especially when the cost of doing it is so high. One of the costs that I have observed are the various punishments meted out to White people who refuse to uphold the notion of White supremacy. This punishment, weirdly enough, comes from supposed allies and foes alike. And work aside, Tobin is a genuinely good guy who is fun to be around and who agrees with me that if this work doesn't bring joy (in the midst of pain and struggle), we can't do it.

Tobin adds about Regina,

> I know of no one else whom I trust as much to call me out when I make mistakes about issues of race and racism, who has shared and worked through as many controversies, and who is as committed to the long-term struggle despite those setbacks. Regina is constant, true, someone in whom there is no deceit. I never have to be concerned about there being a hidden agenda in my dealings with her. Plus, she is one of the most moving and powerful essay writers and lecturers that I know. But it is the simple fact that she hasn't dropped out or cut off connection when I have messed up that is the greatest gift to our relationship.

The events of the summer of 2020 brought us back into closer and more frequent contact. In the aftermath of George Floyd's murder and the subsequent swelling of attention to police abuse of Black women and men in particular and People of Color in general, both of our speaking schedules expanded exponentially. After Tobin and his wife Cheryl started a new nonprofit, Widerstand Consulting, to bring antiracism training resources through online training to religious groups, libraries, and other nonprofits, we began to collaborate more directly.

Once again, it was as if we had never stopped.

AN ANTIRACIST SPIRITUALITY

This brings us to the topic of an antiracist spirituality.

We chose to start with the narrative of our relationship for two primary reasons. First, all spiritualities are about *stories* if they are about anything at all. Our story with its own particular warp and woof weaves a carpet on which we hope others can walk as they explore their own antiracist journey and the spirituality needed for it. Second, spiritualities are equally about *relationships* if they are about anything at all. A relationship with the divine is, of course, first and foremost manifested in a spiritual walk, but as we move deeper into that kind of movement of the Spirit, we invariably move deeper into the relationships around us. Spiritualities wear skin. And so relationships matter as we develop them.

As we have written this book together, we have identified multiple themes that have been present in our relationship and suggest some insight into how an antiracist spirituality can support the work of dismantling racism. In this, we are by no means unique. If anything, the dynamics of our relationship are all too familiar. Tobin has had to struggle with notions of and a tendency toward taking control, assuming superiority, and stepping toward rather than away from the assumption of privilege and power. Regina exists as Black and a woman in a context that denigrates both identities. But it is in fact the very predictability of our relational dynamic across the Black/White divide that makes our story worth exploring from this perspective.

For the vast majority of the book, we will write from an intersectional perspective but will keep our attention focused on racism and the Black/White experience because that best represents our history as a team. Out of this context—one in which we also claim an uncommon measure of resilience and duration—we simply offer reflections from our work together in hopes of equipping others to walk alongside us in the work that yet remains. In short, stories matter and will figure prominently throughout.

When writing about any kind of identity, precise language is important, especially around names. Naming, as we know, is power, and too many times racist power has been used to confer on people names that they did not choose, and to deny people the power to name themselves. We place a high value on honoring the way that people identify themselves individually and collectively. And yet the nature of language is to evolve and change. Furthermore, all people within one group do not necessarily agree on what names should be used. One of the naming challenges that we faced while writing this book was the use of the fairly new term BIPOC (Black, Indigenous, People of Color). On the one hand, People of Color in our respective circles had begun to use the term as a way to identify themselves and as a way of doing antiracism educating and organizing. And yet some people were unsatisfied with the limitations and misunderstandings around the name; for instance, some folks used it to mean Black, Indigenous, and (other) People of Color. While it identifies the unique historical contexts in the United States of people whose land was stolen and people who were stolen to work that land, it also can seem to overlook the importance of other histories. In this book, while we want to be clear that we are focusing on the Black/White racial binary in particular, we do not want to erase the realities of other People of Color in this country.

And so, while the initial draft of this book used BIPOC, we have chosen not to use it extensively in this book, although we do use it in other spaces.

We will begin by defining what an antiracist spirituality means and telling stories of three individuals who embodied that spirituality. This definitional discussion will then turn to an examination of antiracism and spiritual formation to explore how racism has borne itself out even in the midst of spiritual traditions. To counter that history and present reality, we contend that, more than anything else, an antiracist spirituality is realized in practice more than proclamation.

The first three chapters of this book explore the themes of culture and identity. We examine the multiple ways in which anti-Blackness is expressed in culture, society, and the church while also pointing to the Blackness-embracing practices that counter it. Chapter 4 offers ten ideas for engaging with popular culture from a position of antiracist spirituality. Here, we articulate and describe those elements of an antiracist spirituality that speak to one of the most powerful and formative—if frequently unexamined in a spiritual context—forces shaping those of us living and moving in the twenty-first century. We then turn to an exploration of identity and how it connects with spirituality, culture, and Whiteness. We are indeed shaped by racial forces in society. Those forces are powerful but do not have to be, in the end, determinative.

After these exploratory and more theoretical chapters on the most foundational and expansive elements of an antiracist spirituality, we start to apply it. Chapter 7 addresses the centrality of struggle, conflict, and crisis in the work of antiracism and what that means for an antiracist spirituality. As our story demonstrates, we cannot engage in the work of dismantling racism without encountering conflict in some form. The question, then, is not whether that conflict will emerge but how and in which fashion we will bring spiritual resources to bear on it. Here, we will also explore antiracism and the reality of loss and historical trauma and how a mature spiritual walk speaks to those realities.

In chapter 8, we turn to the spiritual work of institutional transformation, building particularly on the contributions of Walter Wink and his examination of the principalities and powers. We reflect on and develop the learnings we bring from our work at dismantling racism in predominantly White institutions through Roots of Justice (formerly Damascus Road) and Widerstand Consulting. In addition to offering guidance on key principles for that work, we show how an antiracist spirituality can embolden, empower, and make those efforts more effective.

We follow our focus on institutions with our assessment of one of the fundamental divides between Black and White communities when addressing racism: the articulation of individual versus communal approaches to racial issues. In much of the same manner as when engaged in the work of dismantling institutional racism, an antiracist spirituality offers key insights into refocusing, reframing, and reconceiving how we approach the issue of racism from the start.

We conclude this book with two final conversations. First, we offer reflections on antiracism and the spiritual disciplines in which we pay particular attention to the ways we can remain grounded, engage in self-care, and stay in the struggle for the long haul. Discussions of resilience and White fragility will figure prominently here. Finally, in our conclusion we have a conversation in which we return to the themes of racial identity and connect them with relationship, sustainable struggle, the importance of breathing, historical trauma, and creating spaces of mutual recognition and support. We close with a coda that offers some final words on the pursuit of an antiracist spirituality.

GRIEF AND JOY

In the summer of 2005, we joined hundreds of other Damascus Road alumni and participants in Atlanta for a ten-year anniversary gathering of that organization's antiracism work in the Anabaptist community. At the evening kickoff, the two of us shared the podium to reflect on our work together in cofounding that institution. We spoke of the struggles we had faced, honored the People of Color and White mothers and fathers in the church who had done the pathbreaking work of naming the church's racism long before we ever showed up on the Mennonite and Brethren in Christ scene, and named our hopes for the future. We talked about needing both love and systemic analysis in the work of dismantling racism. Although we were not yet using the term *spirituality* in our address, we had been using the term *antiracism* for the better part of a decade.

In rereading our notes for the evening's talk, one comment stuck out. We said at that time, "Our work together has been marked by deep grief and intense joy joined at the hip. And yet, we have walked through this history together with both of those legs supporting us."

Grief and joy seem like fitting words to conclude this introduction. An antiracist spirituality, if it is going to be good for anything—anything at all—needs to be good for sitting with grief and fostering joy.

In this book, we promise to do both.

Chapter 1

What Is an Antiracist Spirituality?

I (Tobin) knew that something was awry the first evening when we finished reiterating what we had announced in all the advanced materials. Because of the way the training experience built upon itself, full-time participation was required. We knew from experience that it simply didn't work for participants to drop in for part of the workshop, leave, and come back. Not only was it disruptive to the training experience, but those who dropped in and out invariably asked questions or made comments that flipped us back to material that we had already covered. When several participants explained that they would be attending only parts of the training, we asked that they join us at a future time and explained that it wouldn't work to attend only parts of the event.

When predominantly White institutions are in crisis, when they feel threatened and destabilized, comments and requests *that might not otherwise gain the slightest notice can trigger disproportionate responses. Such was the case in this training.*

Midway through the first day, when we had reviewed little more than a definition of racism that brought both prejudice and power to bear and discussed the historical roots of the idea of race itself, one group of participants had walked out of the training because we had required full-time participation and declared that we were being inflexible. Our immediate supervisor—a Latina woman—was closeted in a conference room with a handful of White male administrators from other parts of the organization, trying to keep them from canceling the entire training on the spot. And a smaller group of participants remained in the room having brought books, articles, and written memos to refute, interrupt, and object to the content we then attempted to provide on White privilege, White supremacy, and the twin dynamics of internalized racial oppression and internalized racial superiority.

I can remember standing in the hallway just outside the fellowship hall after doing my best to respond with some measure of equanimity and grace to a phalanx of White men who stormed up to me at the announced refreshment break to object to statements I had made about how the systems of racism in our country afford unearned advantage to those of us who are White about which we remain unaware. I glanced down the hallway to the narthex, saw the green hills of sub- urban Akron outside, and wanted desperately to run away. In one of the more adult things I had done up to that point in my life, I finished my lemon bar, took another sip of punch, and instead walked back into the training room.

By the time the training neared completion, only a remnant remained. The orientation leaders had given permission for the new volunteers to skip the rest of the training entirely. Many of the organization's headquarters staff simply didn't return, having become frustrated with the controversy that had already erupted. As we prepared to make our closing remarks to a group that was by that point openly hostile to anything that we had to say, an alarm began wailing in the distance.

It was a tornado warning. The sky had turned a sickly shade of green.

And so we filed out of the fellowship hall and pressed ourselves into a basement Sunday school room, where we stood cheek by jowl, uncertain of what would come next. As the sky turned even darker, so did the mood in the room. None of us wanted to be together anymore, let alone crammed together in such close confines.

At some point one of us led out in prayer. A few joined in. Not everyone. But some. I don't remember verbalizing my prayer before the group. It's possible that I did. Mostly I remember wanting it all to just be done.

The sirens eventually stopped. No tornados had touched down in our vicinity. The training was finished.

We never again completed an antiracism analysis orientation training for the staff and volunteers of the relief and development organization Mennonite Central Committee. By the fall of 2010, Damascus Road left MCC and became its own nonprofit, Roots of Justice. The seeds of that departure were sown at that tornado training.

Although the connection may not be immediately evident, this story has everything to do with defining an antiracist spirituality. The antiracist spirituality we offer in this book reminds us that if we are ever going to be successful in tearing down the mansions of White supremacy, we are going to have to move through conflict, past perceived slights, and forward to a beckoning future amid challenging conversations and events just like the tornado training. An antiracist spirituality keeps us grounded in the work that we need to do while we learn from past efforts but helps us not become defined by them. The nature of the struggle itself, the reckoning that such events require, and the measured compassion called for in response embody the best of an antiracist spirituality.

Before offering a definition in full, however, three short vignettes of elders in the movement demonstrate how others have embodied, lived out, and drawn on the very kind of antiracist spirituality we articulate here. One comes from Black freedom struggle leader Fannie Lou Hamer. A second is from another leader in the same struggle, Medgar Evers. A final story comes to us from a White woman who also fought for racial justice, Anne Braden. Their examples define the very nature of an antiracist spirituality.

FANNIE LOU HAMER

Fannie Lou Hamer stood in the nation's spotlight after her appearance on the credentialing committee at the 1964 Democratic National Convention in Atlantic City, New Jersey. She had come to testify about the beating she received in a jail in Winona, Mississippi, after attempting to get Black people to register to vote. As a representative of the Mississippi Freedom Democratic Party (MFDP), Mrs. Hamer had come along with other members of the MFDP to document the systematized efforts to disenfranchise Mississippi's Black population, demonstrate that they had elected their own delegates independent of the established Democratic Party, and demand seats at the table.

Her testimony proved so threatening to President Lyndon B. Johnson that he called a spontaneous press conference to interrupt the networks' coverage of her testimony. Despite her powerful voice, authoritative presence, and reams of documentation, the MFDP did not gain the seats that they sought. Nonetheless, Mrs. Hamer persisted. She ran for statewide office. She organized and raised money for the Mississippi Freedom Farm Cooperative. Even when younger members of the Student Nonviolent Coordinating Committee (SNCC) deemed her "irrelevant," she did not despair. Despite failing health and a rigorous travel schedule, she continued to give leadership to the Freedom Farm Cooperative until just before her passing in 1977 from breast cancer at the age of fifty-nine.

Throughout her work in the Black freedom struggle, Mrs. Hamer invited people to remember who they were and how they could move forward by drawing them into song. The spirituals that she led people in might have been nothing more than vibrations of saccharine sanctity. But she refused to let them be empty gestures. Instead, the songs became both sources of strength and amplifiers of the same. In the singing of "This Little Light of Mine," she invited people to identify both the reach and limits of their work, to join with people around them in collective efforts, to take time to pause from the demands of organizing and resisting and just sing.

Fannie Lou Hamer embodied an antiracist spirituality. She offered the strength born of her faith tradition to those with whom she worked. In many ways, her work and witness were themselves the best evidence of the moment of why and how such a spiritual tradition mattered. One moment in particular captures the strength she found in her antiracist spirituality. While recovering from the beating she received in the Winona jail, Mrs. Hamer stayed with a group of Mennonites in Atlanta. Rosemarie Harding and her husband Vincent hosted dozens of civil rights activists at a voluntary service headquarters known as Menno House in Atlanta just around the corner from where Coretta and Martin King were then living in the early 1960s.

Rosemarie remembered that Mrs. Hamer told Vincent, "You know, if it hadn't been for you I wouldn't have got in all that trouble!" Rosemarie added, "Her face was all swollen. She could hardly speak. Her eyes were mostly closed. And yet she could joke and laugh and her spirit was just wonderful."[1]

Such is the legacy of an antiracist spirituality in action. In the painful aftermath of a violent struggle, joy and laughter bubbled up. Humor ruled the day. Although much struggle lay ahead, in that moment Mrs. Hamer's spirituality offered a way forward.

MEDGAR EVERS

Historian Charles Payne notes that civil rights activist Medgar Evers "commanded more respect than just about anyone else in the Mississippi movement."[2] In his work as the Mississippi field secretary for the NAACP from 1954 through to his death in 1963, Evers fought for full voting rights, fair employment, and an end to all practices of segregation. Like fellow activists Aaron Henry and Amzie Moore, Evers brought his experience as a sergeant in World War II to bear on his organizing efforts in terms of both his ability to motivate volunteers to action and his awareness of a larger world outside of Mississippi in which democracy was fully exercised. On June 12, 1963, Byron De La Beckwith assassinated Evers as Evers walked from his car to his home. But the manner of his martyrdom is not in and of itself a sign of an antiracist spirituality in motion. His assassination was the result of a cowardly act of terrorism conducted by an avowed White nationalist.

We include Evers here not because of how he died but because of how he lived. We lift him up because he was courageous. In 1946 after serving with distinction on the battlefields of Normandy and returning safely home, he and his brother Charles successfully registered to vote, only to face a mob on election day. The group of angry White men denied them "the franchise."[3] Evers remembered feeling intimidated. But despite that initial fear and in the face of further threats of violence that only mounted as his influence grew and he became more effective in his organizing work, he remained faithful in every sense of the word.

Drawing on the spiritual formation he received from his mother, Jesse, a devout member of the Church of God in Christ, and his own participation in a local Baptist congregation, Evers was constant, he was strong, and he did not back down. In a setting where he could at any point be physically attacked and where the very presence of his body in public spaces risked verbal assault, he continued to find the strength to attend rallies, organize local communities, and strategize for long-term change. His spiritual foundation emboldened his action.

ANNE BRADEN

Like Fannie Lou Hamer and Medgar Evers, Anne Braden also remained constant and committed throughout her entire life. Like them, she also drew on a robust spirituality, in her case born of her early participation in the Episcopal tradition. We lift her up here as an example of how a White person integrated an antiracist spirituality into her work as a co-struggler alongside the Black community.

Braden and her husband Carl entered the national stage through an invitation from Andrew and Charlotte Wade in 1954. Because of the racist real estate practices commonplace throughout the South in general and Louisville, Kentucky, in particular, the Wades, who were Black, had not been able to purchase a home in the all-White suburb of Shively. The Wades asked the Bradens to purchase the home and then resell it to them. Anne and Carl agreed. Once they moved in to the house, Andrew and Charlotte and their children faced violence from their White neighbors who not only shot out windows and burned a cross in their front lawn but dynamited the house six weeks after the Supreme Court ended legalized segregation by issuing the ruling in *Brown vs. Board of Education of Topeka, Kansas*. Ultimately the Wades had to sell their house and relocate to a Black neighborhood on the west side of Louisville, and although the White neighbors who planted the dynamite were known and identified, the authorities instead chose to prosecute Carl for his alleged organizing of the integration effort.[4]

In the aftermath of these high-profile events, Anne and Carl could not find employment locally so they began working for the Southern Conference Educational Fund, a small civil rights organization formed to garner financial support for civil rights efforts from White southerners. In the years that followed, Anne Braden would become, according to historian Sara M. Evans, "the most important adult White woman to young southern activists throughout the sixties."[5] Born in the embrace of White southern upper-class gentility, Braden inspired and supported other White people to fulfill, in her words, "the job of white people who believe in freedom . . . to confront white America."[6] White activists like Bob Zellner have credited Braden for mentoring them and guiding them into the work of the freedom struggle.

For her entire adult life, Braden continued to exemplify and model how to live a life of integrity as a White antiracist co-struggler. In 2005, only a year before she passed away at the age of eighty-one, she wrote, "In every age, no matter how cruel the oppression carried on by those in power, there have been those who struggled for a different world. I believe this is the genius of humankind, the thing that makes us half divine: the fact that some human beings can envision a world that has never existed."[7] An antiracist spirituality is built on the foundation of that "half" divinity. Like Anne Braden, we recognize that the divine dwells in all of us and is best expressed when we are engaged in the struggle for a different world based on the active envisioning of an established order that has not yet been and has not yet come about. Anne Braden imagined the possibility of a world different from her own and sought to bring it to fruition.

An antiracist spirituality is not the end-all. It is not the point itself. Too often we confuse the preparation for the work of antiracism with the actual work of antiracism. In a recent training with the board of a directors of an international mission agency, a Black board member challenged his White colleagues to stop doing antiracism trainings if they were only going to do them to say that they had done them. "I am tired of watching organizations like our own only attend to racism when the cameras are flashing and the video recorders are rolling," he said. "Do something or don't do something, but stop pretending that the trainings are themselves the work of antiracism." In the same way, a book purporting to offer an antiracist spirituality is only as good as the results it emboldens, strengthens, and sustains.

In the chapters that follow, we have done our best to offer a way forward. We believe that sharp analysis, compelling stories, and thoughtful reflection can help support and develop a movement to finally make some headway at uprooting racism in our society. Much of what we present comes from our work together and from our collaboration with others both within and without religious communities. In doing so, we stand on so many shoulders of those who have gone before us. Mrs. Hamer, Evers, and Braden are only three examples of those inspiring elders. We will name others in chapters to come.

DEFINING AN ANTIRACIST SPIRITUALITY

Stories of an embodied antiracist spirituality are one thing. Defining it is another. So what is an antiracist *spirituality*? Put simply, a spirituality is a way of addressing matters of faith and religion without using those words, of speaking of the divine but not putting God in a box. It is a category for discussing one's growth and development and maturity that doesn't turn on rote proclamations of salvation or brittle declarations of ideology. A spirituality is a fluid phrase that invites in the seekers and the dabblers and the suspicious who do not trust or have no patience for structured church but seek out connection with that Something that is bigger and broader and more expansive than psychology and culture and sociology says that it has any right to be. But it is also patient with those steeped in the traditional patter of liturgy, ecclesiology, ritual, and creed.

A spirituality is a condition as much as it is a practice. It is a way of being even as it is a chosen discipline. It is shaped by theology but not limited to it.

And what then is an *antiracist* spirituality? It is, at least in this instance, a written companion for those seeking comfort, direction, insight, and instruction to sustain the long-term work of dismantling racism in all its forms. It is a resource to sustain the struggle, invite growth, and help us figure out how to be humans who refuse to give in to White supremacist power, who learn how to love with integrity, and who are authentic in our work and our witness. Racism gets in the way of all these efforts. This antiracist spirituality, we hope, will help get racism out of the way.

AN ANTIRACIST SPIRITUALITY AT WORK: THE TORNADO TRAINING

The story of the tornado training that opens this chapter offers a way to think through how an antiracist spirituality can shape our actions. Just as Mrs. Hamer's, Evers's, and Braden's spiritualities shaped their actions, so too has an antiracist spirituality shaped ours.

First, we note that the greater the power and prestige, the more difficult the work and therefore the greater the need for spiritual resources. At the time of the tornado training, Mennonite Central Committee had a larger budget, employed more staff and volunteers, and encompassed greater connections across the Anabaptist community than any other organization within the Mennonite family of churches in the United States, Canada, or worldwide. No wonder, then, that a challenge to its culture, organizational structure, and way of being would engender such resistance. For an organization that size, there would have been much to gain if we would have been more successful in helping draw the organization to a more antiracist identity and commitment. But there would be much to lose, too.

In the midst of that struggle, we learned to turn to our spiritual tradition as a source of strength and sustenance. We took time to examine our motives and attitudes. We continued to reach out to those who claimed our work was theologically bankrupt. We listened as carefully as we knew how to discern where the Spirit was next leading us.

But we also learned over time to reject the proposition that we were somehow at fault for the reactivity we encountered.

To be certain, this is not to suggest that we were infallible. Over time, we have learned how to respond to overt antagonism in ways that have a better chance of keeping the training on track. We no longer allow facilitators to lead workshops for organizations at which they are employed. And we have a better understanding of the type, sequence, and severity of crises that emerge when predominantly White organizations are being challenged on their racism.

And we have grown older. There's some chance we have grown wiser too. But regardless of our maturity levels, we also know that the events that unfolded did not arise from personal failings on our part. To claim that we were somehow personally at fault for the events that took place would be, in essence, to state that racism is just about interpersonal dynamics. Under that belief, if we repair the relationship, then we repair the problem.

An antiracist spirituality has helped us realize just how much of a lie that is. It has given us the grounding we need to understand the dynamics that unfolded in an event like the tornado training so that we can pick ourselves up, assess the damage, and begin to rebuild without collapsing and throwing up our hands in despair.

Second, one of the most important resources offered by the kind of antiracist spirituality that we promote here is the ability to analyze such events and bring them to a reckoning. The best of the traditions of spiritual formation have long called for clear-eyed reckoning of both personal and corporate failing. The best of those traditions have not engaged in emotional or physical flagellation but rather named those failings directly and with utmost candor. Those traditions have then invited a fresh response, all the while recognizing that both humans and institutions are slow to change, that they need proper support to do so, and that spiritual sustenance can make that long-term work possible. The Ignatian tradition of the examen and the spiritual exercises, the Enneagram, and the vision quest of many Native American communities—these all reflect a similar emphasis on laying bare one's ego, recognizing the traps of self-delusion and collective delusion, and stepping on to a path that is as difficult as it is true.

We think that the events of the tornado training in particular and our work with MCC more generally were so tumultuous because the organization had never come to terms with the depth of its failings or its promise. As has been the case for many predominantly White organizations, the history of its formation has shaped and set up its present practice. Historian Ben Goossen has laid bare how MCC participated in the resettlement of Nazi sympathizers and activists and employed some of the same while crafting a false narrative that covered over those Mennonites' participation in Nazi enterprises.[8] We have also noted within MCC a kind of false modesty that bristles when recipients of the organization's service projects reject the notion that they are in need of aid from well-meaning outsiders. Widespread colorblind rhetoric, a refusal to criticize other White Mennonite institutions, and programs that supported White Mennonite youth while marginalizing youth of color made authentic antiracism work all the more difficult.

Such clear-eyed reckoning is never an easy process. We have at times been tempted to publicly expose the racism of a group we were working with rather than support them to name that for themselves. There have been times when a more direct intervention did prove necessary. We will discuss these elsewhere in this book. But at this juncture, suffice it to say that the decision to intervene has required the best of our spiritual discernment to determine when, how, and under what circumstances to do so.

Finally, an antiracist spirituality challenges us to unify clear-eyed reckoning with measured compassion. Note that we write "measured." We do so because we have observed how quickly White individuals and the institutions that they populate speak of forgiveness and mercy when their participation in racism is pointed out. We again note that turning to forgiveness without reckoning with justice and reparation inevitably leads to a cheap grace, one that does not persist, makes matters worse down the road, and covers over rather than reveals. By contrast, a measured compassion does not jump to the reconciliation moment. It rather sits with the pain, alienation, and record of hurt, damage, and ongoing impoverishment that participation in racism perpetuates. It does not ask for grace in the moment of reckoning. But it does recognize that we are all human—that we have limits on what we can or cannot do. Measured compassion births a wisdom to find the middle way.

Which brings us back to our previous claim that the story of the tornado training shows an antiracist spirituality at work. We've already explored the connections between that tumultuous event and the components of antiracist spirituality. These components include recognizing the correlation between the level of power and the degree of difficulty in dismantling racism, understanding such conflict, providing the strength to weather such storms, and offering both clear-eyed reckoning and a measured compassion. But there is also a central disconnect between this story and the idea of an antiracist spirituality. It has to do with this notion of calling.

One of Tobin's friends recently asked him what he meant when he said that he felt called to do something. This friend,

Linda Karell, who is also a professor in Montana, has no religious affiliation or interest in adopting one. But she was genuinely curious why Tobin had referenced on social media that the Spirit had led him to confess his reluctance to depend on God's providence. She did not understand what this notion of "calling" or "leading" meant. So she asked whether this experience of the Spirit was like the "pain in the butt feeling/voice/knowledge" that she feels when faced with the option to do what is familiar, comfortable, and makes her look "smart, informed, and helpful." Rather than take the safe route, however, that feeling says, "Naw, dude, we're taking this risk, and here we go; look, we're already in the middle of it." She explained, "Because I don't know *spirit* from a wide assortment of vegetables, but that experience I know." And she added, "And at any rate, I love you."

Yes, Linda, that is exactly what we mean by leading. A calling is just a more intense version of the same that connects with more sustained and focused action over a longer period of time. (And love you to the moon and back, sister.)

The disconnect with the experience of the tornado training and the narratively presented definition of antiracism that we are exploring at this juncture is that the event in Akron, for all its conflict and high drama, was in the end as unimportant as it was essential. It was unimportant because racism shows up constantly in the world in which we live. That it would show up in the context of a predominantly White organization is neither unusual nor remarkable. But it was simultaneously essential because all work is local work, and we can only ever really respond with effectiveness in those communities we call our own. Moreover, conducting that training in that highly volatile context was exactly the kind of work that we were being called to do at that time. But—and this exception is the crux of the matter—an antiracist spirituality reminds us that traumatic experiences can become unhealthy fixations of those who survive them. To use language from our spiritual tradition, the process of revisiting the trauma itself can become an idol. We can become stuck in the past, licking old wounds, keeping them open and raw by reminding ourselves of just how awful it was back in the olden days.

While not allowing us to ignore the past, an antiracist spirituality calls us forward.

Developing and telling the narratives of our history is essential for the formation of community. The tornado training has become a touchstone in our work together, a reminder of how things can spiral out of control when one dares to open up conversations about and take on racism. There are no guarantees that the work will move forward without these kind of crises. But we have also learned to let that event go.

WHERE THE STRUGGLE TAKES US

Iris de León-Hartshorn, a longtime co-struggler, friend, coauthor, and former supervisor, wrote this of the work we did together within the context of Mennonite Central Committee:

> We consistently received pressure from some within MCC to focus on work on interpersonal relationships rather than on systemic issues, because white people were more comfortable discussing interpersonal relationships rather than confronting their own white privilege and the systemic barriers that kept white people in control, not just in society but within church institutions as well, including Anabaptist institutions.[9]

In the context of struggling against racism, we need to ask ourselves how we can draw on ever deeper wells of sustenance and strength. How can we state clearly, as de León-Hartshorn has in her assessment of the good, the bad, and the ugly, the barriers that have existed, that continue to exist, that will be ongoing? How can we listen to what the Spirit is calling us to do, draw on spiritual resources to answer that calling, and at the same time recognize that the very notion of calling itself has been used to hide behind clear-eyed assessment of one's participation in racist practices? Spiritual discernment is indeed necessary.

And part of that discernment requires a clear understanding of what we mean by an antiracist spirituality. Thus, a final definition is in order: An antiracist spirituality is a way of being in the world that draws on the unknown and unknowable—which some call Spirit, others name the divine, goes by the word of Mystery, relates to us as God—to encourage, empower, and enthuse amid the intention and the action to undermine the systems of White supremacy around us. It is marked by knowledge of the warp and woof of race-based power, privilege, and oppression. It fosters truth-telling—first to self and then to others. It lifts up communal efforts, is not afraid of hard conversation, and invites laughter, joy, and human connection. An antiracist spirituality encourages awareness of limitation while inviting all that has not yet been conceived, gestated, or birthed to move into the possible and be fully realized. It is strong. It does not demand perfection. It does not easily crumble.

In the early years of our work together, the steering committee that guided our efforts—a delightful collection of church leaders, grassroots organizers, and longtime activists that was by design made up of a majority of People of Color—laid hands on us and prayed that we would remain faithful in the work, that we would not grow weary, and that we would persevere. Their touch—both physical and emotional—buoyed us through some of the most challenging days of our collaboration when we were just figuring out how to trust each other even as multiple forces, many of them inside the very church community that we were attempting to call to faithfulness, aimed to dismiss our efforts before they had an opportunity to start.

The witness of that community is one of the best examples of a collective expression of antiracist spirituality that we know. Tangible, defined by celebration, willing to struggle, united in common understanding, unafraid to name and challenge White supremacy at every turn, and always listening for what unexpected leading the Spirit would draw us to this time. They were the fire that fought the fire sweeping down upon us.

With gratitude for their witness we are now able to offer this understanding of antiracist spirituality in all its manifestations to you.

Use it well.

It has been born of much struggle. It has been watered with many tears. It has been graced with peals of laughter.

Chapter 2

Antiracism and Spiritual Formation

Jesus loves the little children . . .
Red and yellow, black and white,
they are precious in his sight.
Jesus loves the little children of the world.

I (Regina) learned (and sang) this song in Sunday school as a child, and it actually reflected our congregation's reality as a multiracial church. I was a child during the 1960s, when the news was infused with reports about racial unrest, the civil rights movement, and the Vietnam War. For a while, I thought being Christian meant being against racial oppression and war. Well, I still think and believe that—when I was a kid I thought every Christian believed that, and that's why we learned this song.

Eventually I learned other ways that Christians viewed race, and how it could and did show up in policies and legislation that affected people's lives, as it did in the indictment regarding the marriage of Mildred and Richard Loving, an interracial couple:

> Almighty God created the races white, black, yellow, malay and red, and he placed them on separate continents. And but for the interference with his arrangement there would be no cause for such marriages. The fact that he separated the races shows that he did not intend for the races to mix.[1]

These two sentiments—a children's Sunday school song and a court decision indicting interracial marriage as a felony—acknowledge racial diversity as fodder for theological and ethical contemplation. One declares the love of God for all; the other asserts racial segregation to be the will of God.

In *Black Womanist Ethics*, theologian and ethicist Katie Cannon recalls the start of her exploration of Christian ethics, which would become her life's work. As a young Black girl, she learned the central affirmations of Christianity in the Black church while simultaneously existing in a Black body in a virulently racist country. Cannon sought to make sense of doctrine taught in church while also seeing the suffering, oppressions, and exploitation of Black people. As a scholar, Cannon continued to ponder Black suffering and the way Christian ethics assumed choice and self-direction: to (willingly) suffer was dutiful, a voluntary, vocational pledge of cross-bearing.[2] But for African Americans, suffering in a brutal racial caste system was not voluntary. What did Christian ethics and theology have to say about that?

Cannon used narrative to explore this paradox, using stories from the lived experience of Black people, and Black women specifically. Her goal was to understand ethics and moral choices under oppression, the realities that shaped the context in which Black women made moral judgments and ethical choices. This inquiry led to a body of work that helped legitimize the critical importance of marginalized perspectives and voices in the field of ethics, and that also served as a foundation on which to build resistance to oppression. Cannon and others clearly articulated the problem with ethical and theological scholarship and ecclesial practice that did not acknowledge the existence of marginalized and oppressed people. Where we are situated matters.

We cannot extract an understanding of how identity is formed without acknowledging race as a meta-narrative of U.S. identities, forged along a Black/White binary. Our inherited history successfully reinvents itself generation after generation. Socialization in a racist context affects how we think and what we create, therefore spilling over into our theologies and spiritual formations.

In order for faith communities to have genuine, sustained conversations about race, they must understand White supremacy and its effects, which have driven economics, politics, and other systems that Black people must encounter and navigate daily. Racism, and other isms that marginalize, harm, and destroy people, must also be named as sin.

If we are able to have that kind of honest talk about what White supremacy is and how it destroys, we can begin to identify how it functions within our systems: our denominations, our mission boards, our schools, and our congregations. It is one thing to do an analysis and have a head knowledge of White supremacy, and quite another to face it in our own house. But this kind of understanding is necessary to support the fostering of an antiracist future, because then our plans and strategies can begin by asking this question: Does this decision support the notion of White supremacy, or does it negate the notion of White supremacy?

The phrase *White supremacy* might be jarring, and to some might only conjure images of wild-eyed racial terrorists that blatantly commit acts of physical harm upon People of Color. These images could seem easy to discount—those were the bad old days; perhaps there are a few fringe folks in the present, but surely that designation does not include anyone who would seek out a book about antiracist spirituality. However, the notion of White supremacy that we are using here is simply this: the cultural idea that White people are, well, just better people. Racist policies and practices are held in place by cultural ideas that say White people are more human, are more civilized, more capable of self-governance, and more deserving of the better things in life (housing, jobs, education, etc.). White supremacy supposes that White people should be trusted more without having to do anything to earn that trust except to show up. Insidious in nature, it is profoundly damaging spiritually.

White supremacy/racism's wiliest trick is to pretend it doesn't exist.

RACISM ENDED . . . RIGHT?

I (Regina) have had lots of conversations with well-meaning White people that lift up two seemingly unrelated but connected themes: (1) explaining that racism isn't really a thing anymore, and (2) asserting that because of that, Black people no longer have a distinctly different way of experiencing life in this country. These two ideas work together to support colorblindness as the way forward—because we are all the same, and we just need to learn to love one another. This is the sentiment expressed in the Sunday school song quoted at the beginning of the chapter. Since Jesus loves all the children, no matter their skin color, Jesus followers should do the same. The way to do that is to treat everyone the same; we don't need to upend systems or change the way our society is structured. Absent historical context, it can make sense. But it doesn't answer the questions a young Katie Cannon was asking: If our churches teach love, why does racial hatred exist? A colorblind approach in the context of unacknowledged White supremacy and anti-Blackness makes Black people a problem to be fixed. It centers Whiteness and White culture as the norm to which everyone should ascribe.

So in these conversations, people (upon learning what I do) try to convince me that the solution to racial tension is very simply racial groups being willing to spend time with one another so that we could understand each other better. Their examples usually come from their own experience of meeting People of Color (usually in predominantly White settings), being nervous and maybe a little prejudiced at first, but then getting to know them and realizing that they were just fine people. And for them, that erases any bit of racism they personally had.

Some years ago, I spoke in a church in the rural Midwest. During a break I was talking with a few folks and we were sharing stories about our families and our kids. With one of the stories I shared, I thought it would be helpful to explain code-switching as I talked about the way I talked with my children at home that often differed from the way we spoke in public. The broader point that I was trying to make was how code-switching is a strategy African Americans and other People of Color use to fit into the White norm in order to be considered professional and intelligent. The other point

I was making was about Black culture—our language and its grammar.

One woman got really engaged in a back-and-forth with me about how she did the same thing with her kids and so she really didn't think that it was unique or specific to Black people. The conversation became especially frustrating when I realized how invested this woman was in making me understand that our experiences were the same, and that I was therefore wrong. She saw nuclear family bonding, while I understood code-switching as family bonding, a unique way of knowing and being in the Black diaspora, and a means of survival. Code-switching extends beyond the walls of our home—it's how Black people say "I see you" across the room to someone you've never met to acknowledge your connection.

She really dug in her heels, and I finally let it go. But it bothered me, so much so that I remember it at least two decades later. For some reason, it was critically important for this woman to convince me that we were the same. I sensed in her determination a struggle with cognitive dissonance, that discomfort of holding two very different ideas—a faith narrative that says God loves us all, and we are all created in the image of God, yet we are fundamentally different in ways that mean we should be separate.

The cognitive dissonance of race is expressed by the questions Katie Cannon and James Cone brought to their ethical and theological work: If Christianity teaches of a God who loves all of creation, and commands humans who bear the image of God to love one another, how are we simultaneously divided by difference in ways that visit real harm upon the bodies and psyches of marginalized people, and why have these divisions been sanctioned by the same theology that preaches love?

For many socialized in the United States, understanding about racism and segregation is vastly oversimplified and is watered down to simple misunderstandings and an inherent fear of difference. Beyond the groups of people who have tried to pay attention to the systemic nature of racialized violence, the understanding that racist acts of terror are grounded in some strains of Christian theology goes unnoticed and unheeded.

Whiteness as the norm makes racial identity less salient for White people. Even though critical race theory and Whiteness studies have increased an understanding of the existence of White identity, that salience is still not as present for White people until their Whiteness is brought into sharp relief by proximity with Blackness.

An antiracist spirituality affirms that the image of God resides within all of humanity. Racialized hierarchies deny this, and have even denied humanity to Black people in order to justify enslavement, segregation, and criminalization. Many people, including White people who don't think of themselves as racist or as espousing White supremacy, do not realize how powerful the overlay of that system is. It has been, and continues to be, powerful enough to drive the U.S. economy. As we have noticed on multiple social media platforms, it is also powerful enough to convince people that having a Black- or Brown-skinned person at the top levels of government is a sure sign of the decline of that government. Consciously working against systems of oppression like racism—that is, being antiracist—recognizes that what is good for the people at the bottom of the hierarchy is ultimately good for everyone.

Segregation did not happen accidentally; it is the result of a number of interlocking and colluding public and business policies. It is the result of people agreeing with public policy to the extent that segregation is held in place. Our churches carry on the tradition of segregation in part because of the legacy of residential segregation, but even more so because of the history of Christianity's participation in the oppression of African Americans. To seek "diversity" without facing this history is difficult. Multiracial worshiping communities do exist; however, these are not predominantly White churches with a handful of People of Color, or the reverse. The measure, according to sociologist Michael Emerson, is when no more than 60 percent of the membership belongs to one racial group.[3]

An ethnographic study by sociologist Gerardo Martí of a large (average attendance 1,400) multiethnic church illustrates why it is difficult for African Americans in particular to participate in these churches, especially if they are in the minority.[4] The study looked at the beliefs, attitudes, and behaviors that promoted diversity within the congregation. Racially conscious African Americans who bring their Black realities and concerns are dissatisfied and often do not stay in such congregations. This is because many multiracial/diversity efforts require people to "transcend" race; their Christian identity is expected to overshadow other identities, including race and ethnicity. This was the case for congregants in Martí's study, something that is not an option for Black people in the United States.[5] It is not that the African Americans in the study took their Christian identities less seriously than the others; rather, African American identity is more difficult to not be cognizant of. Those who left could not, and would not, subsume their Black identities, which informed the way they moved about in the world.

In part, this is the double consciousness articulated by W. E. B. Du Bois; one's awareness of the world as one sees and experiences it is one level of consciousness. The other consciousness is an awareness of the way the world sees you (often critically) and therefore influences how you operate and act. As an example, the criminalization of Blackness makes Black people hyperaware of being followed in stores or in White neighborhoods, and they may adjust their behavior accordingly by not carrying large bags, or having hands in pockets, or even going into neighborhoods that are unsafe for them to be in. The "driving while Black" phenomenon morphed into "existing while Black," and more and more instances of Black people being harassed or killed for being in the wrong neighborhood or other place give evidence to this.

A church committed to antiracism must equip itself by recalling stories of racialization—how did people become "raced," and what does that mean in the U.S. context? What does it mean for Anabaptist Christians and the way they perceive the power of the gospel in the aftermath of segregation? Such questions begin the necessary introspection for a monocultural congregation that is exploring intentional change or trying to deepen conversations within a racially diverse community.

That familiar Sunday school song reminds us that the notion of racial/ethnic difference is mentioned, even in monoracial settings.

Red and yellow, Black and White
They are precious in his sight . . .

The stories of Jesus' ministry and the stories of the early church show us conscious and deliberate uses of familial language that disrupts the power of the empire. Jesus heals a woman and calls her daughter. Paul addresses the worshiping communities under his care as siblings. In their context, these are also political terms. Jesus and the early church leaders were fostering a new system of relatedness among God's created human order. They are reenvisioning it, because as the Hebrew Scriptures attest, this was always the intent.

Even so, religious folk have struggled with who is inside and who is outside ever since we have tried to belong to God and to one another. From the earliest Christianizing efforts of the slaveholding nation, the church throughout the Americas wrestled with what it meant to be kin to one another. Deeply held racist beliefs were placed alongside Christian beliefs. The two together could not support one another in a sustainable way. Indeed, violent acts of racism were committed and perpetuated and justified by people who understood themselves to be doing God's work in the world. We would not have the deep fissure between Black and White Christians were it not for the church's embodied practices of separation, segregation, and complicity with violence against Black bodies.

Racism's logic works to convince everyone that division and separation are natural, normal, and desirable. Criminalizing Black bodies is one way of supporting this kind of separation, and it also supports the idea that Blackness itself is a sort of curse or punishment. The church has been all too complicit in using theology to reaffirm the racism of the surrounding society.

Just as the U.S. landscape has been shaped by the politics of exclusion, so has the church. It has embodied separation and exclusion while preaching the virtues of togetherness, love, and acceptance. A most visceral reminder of this is Richard Allen, founder of the African American Episcopal Church. Allen was born in 1760 in Philadelphia. He was enslaved at birth, and belonged to a Quaker master. At seventeen, Allen converted to Methodism, eventually bought his freedom, and became a traveling Methodist preacher. He returned to Philadelphia in 1786 and joined St. George's Methodist Church, where he often led prayers. One Sunday morning Allen and other Black parishioners mistakenly sat in pews that had been reserved for Whites. They were told they could not pray there and that they must go up to the balcony. Because they did not move quickly enough, Allen and the others were dragged out of the church.

There has always been resistance to these experiences of exclusion. Yet each step toward liberation has been a hard-won fight, even, and perhaps especially, in our faith communities.

We note that the Black church has been a sanctuary and buffer against racism. It builds and continues a tradition of affirming the humanity of Black people, and it provides a participatory space. Cannon describes the cultural inheritance that was passed down when its participants were under the mantle of slavery and their very bodies were not their own:

> Our ancestors had the hours from nightfall to daybreak to foster, sustain, and transmit cultural mechanisms that enabled them to cope with . . . bondage. In spite of every form of institutional constraint, Afro-American slaves were able to create another world, a counterculture within the White-defined world, complete with their own folklore, spirituals, and religious practices.[6]

For Cannon, these were the cultural windows through which she learned the range of Black response to dehumanization.

In addition to sanctuary, the Black church has been a place of organizing for liberation, and for the transmission of a culture. And it has been a place to mourn. Black people need places to process trauma and grief. When the news cycle and social media outlets are filled with visual and audio records of Black death, when people are reminded over and over again of the expendability of Black life—whether through a study of our history or just reading the news—a place is needed to process. These functions cannot be taken lightly by predominantly White churches that seek to be in community with Black communities.

For many Black people, primary spiritual formation happened in spaces that understood and loved Blackness. This was true for me (Regina), and I learned that my belovedness by God did not need to be sanctioned by White people for it to be authentic. This is important for the vision of antiracist Christian community—can we create interracial, antiracist spaces where Blackness is loved and valued and seen as imaging God?

Is it possible to foster antiracist spirituality that is deliberate and tended to regularly throughout the church year? We think this is Christian formation at a most profound level. It has to be worked at and practiced in the same way that we remember our faith narratives and cycle through the liturgical year.

The other aspect of spiritual formation in an antiracist perspective is the recognition of racism (and other structural oppressions) as sin. When we first started doing antiracism work in the church, we had to be careful about using the language of sin. It wasn't that we didn't believe racism to be sin, but we were mindful of the easy movement from identifying something as sin to understanding it as solely personal sin, the antidote of which is to ask for forgiveness for the personal slights that one may have visited upon someone else. It was already so hard to get people to move away from a definition of racism as a strictly interpersonal enterprise.

So much of American mythmaking has to be undone. So much of our sense of ourselves as exceptional. Undoing racism is a lot of undoing, and those deeply held myths about identity are not easily taken apart. They are not taken apart when they exist within cultural assumptions of anti-Blackness. This is why antiracism must be a practice; a practice in which we (People of Color and White people) are counter to the culture and formed and reformed into the beloved community of God's vision and intent.

If we are trying to understand how the past has created the present in order to shape a different future, it helps to get into the habit of asking three questions:

What happened?

Why did it happen?

What do we do now?

These are the kinds of questions the mystics and seers—the prophets in the biblical texts—used to help the people of God make sense of their current conditions. Prophets, as the mouthpieces of God, spoke uncomfortable truths, but they also spoke words of great comfort. They spoke into specific social, political, and economic contexts, always reminding the people who they were, not only concerning their covenant relationship with God, but also regarding their responsibilities to each other and especially those on the margins. Their words of chastisement and care continued to form and reform God's people in the way of God's radical love and overwhelming justice.

Prophets are still speaking today. They still identify where God's people have missed the mark, and still proclaim a way forward.

Chapter 3

The Spirituality of Embracing Blackness in an Anti-Black Culture

As we mentioned in the introduction, when we first started doing antiracism work, we got a lot of pushback for using the word *racism*. It was too negative, and people were uncomfortable (so we were told) using negative language. Folks would ask, Aren't you ultimately working for something positive? Antiracism is positive—we are working to end racism, and here we are specifically looking at anti-Black racism in the U.S. context.

We suspect there might be similar discomfort with the term *anti-Blackness*. Yet Blackness and darkness are used negatively in a number of contexts, and these associations are also applied to Black and dark-skinned people around the world. For instance, Africa was characterized in the nineteenth century by Europeans as the "dark continent" full of savagery, and was colonized and robbed of resources, including people. This is not just a North American phenomenon; evidence of the market for skin lightening creams and lotions sold around the world, the preference for light-skinned actors and models in entertainment and media, and disparities around employment opportunities and income illustrate the profound distaste for Blackness and Black people—and Blackness in opposition to Whiteness is a critical part of the dynamic.

The Black/White, good/bad dynamic shows up in the language of faith. For Christians, it is in part influenced by contextualized interpretations of the biblical text. The words and images illustrate the choices that lie before us: to be good or to be evil. To be washed "white as snow" or to be cast into utter darkness. Sunday school and church camp craft sessions have taught countless children the story of salvation by using colored beads to represent faith in Jesus (white) and sin (black). Both of us attended Easter morning breakfasts at predominantly White churches that had festive little cups of jelly beans at each place setting—black jelly beans for sin and death and white jelly beans for purity and God's grace.

Some may not be convinced there is a connection, but these few examples (of many more) illustrate the strong relationship between language and attitudes that we believe tell an important story about the development and persistence of anti-Blackness as it concerns Black people. Because we have chosen to think about race and how it functions systemically in the United States, we want to identify the specificity of anti-Blackness in the context of U.S. racism.

This specificity lets us acknowledge the fluidity of language as well as the way that language choices can (intentionally or unintentionally) obfuscate meaning. In our work we focus on the importance of a common language so that we don't talk past one another. However, language evolves, and names for racial categories change. Precision and specificity around language allows us to discuss the history of these kinds of changes while also illustrating the complexity of racial identities. People within the same racial "category" may use different ways of identifying themselves; for instance, one may have a preference for Black over African American.

In the early days of Damascus Road, the antiracism training process we developed, the training teams made serious efforts to regularly include the names of all racial groups instead of always, or only, saying "People of Color." We still believe it is good practice to remain consciously aware and mindful of the truth that diverse and distinct racial groups exist, and that the ways each group will be affected by racism is influenced by their respective, unique histories.

There are times when it is necessary to be precise, and to go deep. As opportunities and spaces are made for more voices to speak about their specific contexts, we know that one voice cannot speak for an entire group. We can both be precise and go deep while continuing to partner and support one another in our desire to work against racism.

Noticing and calling out anti-Blackness does not mean that racism against other groups of People of Color does not exist, and it does not mean that anti-Black racism is what should be given the most attention. Instead, anti-Black racism is a window through which we can understand U.S. racial hierarchies, how they function, and how the culture itself compels everyone to participate in it. Anti-Black racism provides us with a study of how individual, institutional, and cultural racism operate together. Activist, writer, and community organizer Scott Nakagawa helpfully says anti-Black racism is the "fulcrum of white supremacy" in an essay explaining why he, an Asian American man, focuses on Blackness rather than Asian identities for his antiracism work.[1] Anti-Blackness is a phrase that identifies a particular kind of racism embedded in U.S. culture so firmly and for so long that we might just recognize it as "that's what it means to be American."

Anti-Blackness exists in the context of a Black/White binary. Some may wonder why we say the U.S. racial binary is Black and White, and not Indigenous and White. A Black/White binary acknowledges Indigenous erasure, the disregarding of the very presence of Native people, historically and contemporarily. A look at the history of racial categories used by the U.S. census illustrates this erasure; the first census in 1790 had only three "racial" categories: free whites, all other free persons, and slaves. The categories "Indian" and "Chinese" were added in 1870, while from the first census on, people of African descent were identified first as slaves. Later the designations "colored" and "black" appeared. While the option to self-identify as multiracial on the census is recent, the categories of mulatto, quadroon, and octoroon (persons who were one-half, one-quarter, or one-eighth Black) began showing up in 1850.

The very idea of "race" and its existence within a hierarchy began with the notion of race as a way of categorizing people by skin color. Swedish botanist Carl Linnaeus proposed four races of human beings. German physician and naturalist Johann Blumenbach built on Linnaeus's work, arguing for five groups in his *On the Natural Varieties of Mankind* in the late 1700s. Blumenbach arranged the races on a scale, with Caucasians at the top, followed by Mongoloids, Malayans, Ethiopians, and Americans. He then went on to not only classify but quantify: Caucasians were the most beautiful and the original race; all other races were but degenerates of this primary group.

The categories and their attributes provided a handy justification for global exploration and colonization that built and undergirded an economic system that depended on the theft of Indigenous lands in the Americas and the theft of people from the African continent. Black and Brown folks, being "lesser" people, justified the building of systems based on exploitation. We must not underestimate the sheer number of people who had to cooperate with this system in order for it to be beneficial and in continual operation to exist for as long as it did. That cooperation needed authoritative sources (science and religion) blessing the arrangement, a continued stream of rhetoric that socialized people into accepting the arrangement as perpetual and necessary, and sufficient benefits to people with the power to keep the system in place.

The system of racialization especially needed to convince everyone within the system of the supremacy of Whiteness. After the period of enslavement came one hundred years of segregation, during which the Black/White binary forced anyone not in either of those groups to, if they were allowed, choose a side. Some groups were able to earn their way into Whiteness, which generally began with agreeing with the proposition that White people were superior. Those not within the category of White needed to learn what their place was, and to never step out of it on pain of death. Practice became custom, custom became law. Lynching could be the punishment for breaking laws like looking a White person directly in the eyes or not stepping off the sidewalk to let a White person pass.

The persistence of the racial hierarchy is evident in the way it continued to be codified. It showed up in laws against interracial marriage and integrated spaces (restaurants, movie

theaters, public transportation, neighborhoods). It showed
up in popular culture—minstrel shows, published children's
books that freely used the N-word, racist Black memorabilia.
Vestiges remain into the twenty-first century as they are shared
via social media—in racist caricatures of Barack and Michelle
Obama and, more recently, Stacey Abrams.

It's not just that these images and these stories exist; it is
that they continue to shape ideas about who people are and
what is permissible to do to them. The anti-Black campaign,
well over four hundred years old, shows no evidence of slow-
ing down. It exists alongside a culture that celebrates and even
glorifies Black people in specific roles like sports or entertainment, but will quickly chastise them if the boundaries of those
roles are overstepped, such as when NFL quarterback Colin
Kaepernick began taking a knee during the national anthem.

Theological anti-Blackness shows up in bad biblical interpretation. In Genesis 9, we encounter Noah and his sons in the
post-flood world. In a less-well-known narrative than the ark
story, Noah gets falling down drunk. He is also naked. His sons
happen upon him in this state, and one of them is "cursed" for
seeing his father's nakedness. Generations of White Christians
have had this story taught to them as "the curse of Ham" and
as a biblical justification for the enslavement of Africans, the
generational "curse" being dark skin.

These interpretations pairing Blackness and darkness with
negativity, sin, evil, savagery begin in the Bible's origin stories.
Does the biblical text mean to associate dark skin with negative attributes? No. In fact, in the Bible, we also read of darkness being associated with beauty and goodness; it is not only
a descriptor for bad things. However, coupled with teaching
God's blessing of brutal chattel slavery, the linkages (for some)
make sense.

From the era of enslavement on, there is evidence of how important it was to identify any trace of Black ancestry in a person, down to one "drop" of Black blood. Those early census records illustrate how Blackness was detected and categorized—the mulattos, quadroons, and octoroons. The one-drop rule, exclusively applied to Blackness, is a colloquial label for the sociological term "rule of hypodescent." This so-called rule meant that if a person who appeared to be White was known (or found out) to have even one Black person in their family line, that person was considered legally Black. To be considered legally Black meant being excluded from things that White people—free people—had access to.

Psychologist Janet Helms has helpfully theorized about racial identity development among African Americans and notes the effects on Black children being raised in a hostile racialized context—that is, a context that continually demonstrates its undervaluing of Black lives. Helms notes that the self-perception of Black children is influenced by how they are seen and exacts a high cost on their psychological and emotional development. Of course, racism's negative effect on self-image has been well documented. In the 1940s, Kenneth and Mamie Clark conducted their doll experiment, showing Black children between the ages of three and seven dolls who were identical in every way except for having White or Black skin. The children were asked a series of questions: Which doll is the nice doll? Which doll is the pretty doll? Which doll is the bad doll? Which doll is the ugly doll? The Clark doll experiment illustrated how much cognizance even young children had of the positive value placed on Whiteness and the negative value placed on Blackness, and at such a young age. Even before these children may have felt the sting of racism as an impact on their own lives, they had observed the placement of people who look like them in the racial hierarchy, and subsequently internalized an understanding of the world's value on people who look like them. In the Clarks' language, the children knew who was pretty, and who was not. They knew who was smart, and who was not. They knew who would be valued in the world.

In 2005, a sixteen-year-old high school student named Kiri Davis revisited the Clark experiment; she recorded her research and produced an award-winning short film, *A Girl Like Me*. In the film, young Black boys and girls are asked to point to the doll that is pretty/smart or bad/ugly. When asked why the doll is pretty or ugly, the respective answers are "Because she is White" or "Because she is Black." Black children still know who is considered to have worth.

In school, Black youth are often "tracked" into bottom tiers, identified as being lower-performing or lower-intellect students. They receive more and harsher punishments for the same infractions that White students commit, part of the well-documented school-to-prison pipeline.

While mass incarceration and the overrepresentation of Black people in the prison system are becoming better understood, the linkages with how Black youth experience the education system often are not. In 2000, Ann Arnett Ferguson's groundbreaking research studied the effects of institutional racism on the development of Black boys' identities. Ferguson examined how Black boys between fourth and sixth grade were identified as "troublemakers" by those in authority and routinely punished more quickly and more severely for the same infractions committed by White students, male and female, and sometimes Black girls. Ferguson concluded that the Black boys both internalized their identity as troublemakers and acted out as a way of asserting their own autonomy, creativity, and independence.[2]

For centuries, in so many ways, our society at large has learned to distrust, dislike, and demonize Black people. An entire socialization process, firmly rooted in place, teaches anti-Blackness generation after generation. We cannot become antiracist without understanding and facing anti-Blackness. We need to engage in a reformation.

We believe that faith communities have a critical part to play in this because faith communities are the experts at formation. They are where attention is paid to belonging, mutual care, justice, and peace. Promoting all these values is also the work of antiracism and anti-Blackness. White congregations can choose to be explicit about this, and we have models in the Black church, which has had to do this work as a matter of survival. We think it is time for predominantly White churches in particular to be just as engaged. There are models that exist in other institutions that can be instructive.

Regina offers a closing reflection on the role of the Black church in her development.

The rejection of anti-Blackness was modeled to me by the adults in my life at home, at church, and at school. A primary vehicle was the arts. In elementary school, I had a teacher who made us memorize poetry (from the Harlem Renaissance). I remember learning, and then reciting with the rest of my class in a kind of chorus, James Weldon Johnson's "The Creation: A Negro Sermon." I can recall that poem in its entirety, along with Langston Hughes's "Mother to Son" and others. These poems, like the music of the Black church, live in me and connect me to the artists, the time period they were written, and every other person who read and loved and memorized these poems. I pass it on when I can; for instance, I introduce my students to Johnson's version of the creation narrative when we study Genesis.

These artists and so many more created under the towering shadow of a country that dismissed and discounted them. They sang and danced and partied and prayed and created despite what the world gave them. Some of them were poor, others came from families with some means. Some were cautiously invited into White circles, gaining patrons, which allowed them to pursue their art. They argued with each other over the use of dialect in their prose—ever mindful of the White gaze that already thought of them as less than.

They looked at this country and lovingly told the truth about what it was to be a perpetual stranger in the land of your birth but still somehow find joy. They are the carriers of my culture; they are my sacred texts. They bear witness to the struggle to be seen, heard, understood, and valued.

The Black church makes a home for this kind of artistry and activism—it is part of our worship. The association of Black gospel music is familiar (even though the media gets it wrong). The recitation of Black poetry and speeches may be less well known. People make fun of the length of Black church services, but there is a lot that needs to be done. First of all, church was the first institution in this country that we owned. Church was the place you could be called Sister Jones, Brother Franklin, instead of "boy" or "Annie." Church was the place you could hold your head high, knowing you belonged. Church was the place little ones barely old enough to toddle could be up front singing in the children's choir, and even early readers could read Scripture. It was a place where your body could be affirmed in its Blackness—something that didn't happen the other days of the week for many of the congregants.

Chapter 4

Antiracism and Popular Culture

In early introductory antiracism workshops that we did together back in the late 1990s, we would sometimes include a clip from the animated Disney movie *Aladdin*. The original opening lyrics spoke of a faraway land of heat and camel caravans—and how folks would "cut off your ear" if they didn't like the way you looked, a "barbaric" practice, acknowledged the singer, but it was still home. The casual racism proffered by this film and many others emerging from the Disney entertainment factories provided a way into a conversation about racism in popular culture. It does the same thing here.

In this chapter we will explore the complex matrix of identity and culture, examine what that means for the work of seeking an antiracist spirituality, and carefully consider how we engage with popular culture. Movies and fiction will figure prominently, but we will also consider music, art, and fashion.

Within the broad array of popular culture choices before us there is much to consider and address in terms of racism both overt and subtle, much to which an antiracist spirituality can speak. The choices we make about popular culture frequently set the stage for how we approach interracial relationships, conceive of an antiracist future, and work to bring that future to fruition. If we learn how to engage popular culture with integrity, we can be far better equipped to live our antiracist values in our daily lives.

When discerning the kind of popular culture material to include in our workshops, we frequently discussed the relative merits of providing evidence of racism in popular culture versus running the risk of inadvertently reifying and concretizing the very racial stereotypes that we sought to undermine. Did we do harm, for example, by showing a clip from Disney's original 1941 animated film *Dumbo* featuring the flock of black crows who cheer the protagonist on while reenacting the worst of the Jim Crow (yes, that was the name of the lead member of the corvid chorus) minstrelsy tradition? The racism is as clear in that kind of clip as it is in the roustabout scene from the same movie—the only to feature Black people in the cartoon—in which the faceless Black circus laborers sing a song celebrating their semi-enslaved status. Showing evidence from cultural artifacts like these certainly made the point that cultural racism has been widespread, overt, and long-standing, but the very practice of screening them also served to reanimate them, allowing them to do their cultural shaping work.

We eventually stopped projecting evidence of overt racist stereotypes such as those included in the documentary *Ethnic Notions*, a 1987 exploration of the anti-Black stereotypes embedded in popular culture from the pre–Civil War era through the 1960s. Instead, we described and discussed those images without actually bringing them into the training space. The affront of the images themselves, even when brought to bear for critical purposes, was simply too great. We decided that we did not need visual contact with those racist depictions to make our case. Instead, participants could seek out and view those images on their own time if they really needed to be convinced that such racism existed.

That decision did not, however, significantly undermine the great engines of popular culture that seem so mired in and committed to not only perpetuating and marketing overt racist images but supporting the dominance of White superiority. Those processes are powerful and pervasive, often drawing huge audiences. They have proven difficult to change. Precisely because of that influence we feel it is essential to make the connections evident between engaging with an antiracist spirituality and consuming popular culture.

Both of us are fans of and watch movies and plays when we can. Regina loves *The Blues Brothers*. Tobin has screened *The Lord of the Rings* trilogy more times than is probably good for anyone. We have discussed the relative merits of *Hamilton* on more than one occasion (be forewarned—even the slightest hint of disrespect toward this play risks bringing down the wrath of Regina). Life, like popular culture, is meant to be enjoyed.

But we also recognize how the escapism, commercialism, consumerism, and stereotypical elements of much popular culture media—whether films, songs, sports, or fashion—work against the very values we seek out and support through our antiracism work. The question for us is not whether we engage with popular culture but rather how. And so we offer a list of ten ideas—and ten examples—for engaging with those popular culture sources—employing in the process the best of the anti-racist spirituality that we are trying to share in this book.

1. POPULAR CULTURE AFFIRMS WHITE SUPREMACY

The first comment we have to offer is that real work is done through the production of popular culture. It is not just entertainment and frippery. The ways we tell stories, no matter how fanciful or far out, help create the values that determine whose lives are cherished, which cultural traditions are maintained, and whose voices we listen to and whose we ignore. When Peter Jackson made the decision to follow J. R. R. Tolkien's descriptions of good and evil beings in *The Lord of the Rings* saga, he and his production team crafted dark-skinned orcs—the ferocious Uruk-hai in particular—and light-skinned elves, to name only two examples. All his heroes were White and, with one or two exceptions, male. The message was explicit: White lives are normative, White lives are brave, White lives embody goodness. Other examples in film and television abound, such as the all-White leading casts of popular series like *Newhart*, *Everybody Loves Raymond*, *Seinfeld*, *Cheers*, *Sex and the City*, *Family Ties*, and *Frasier*. And when Black characters do appear, they frequently serve the role of the "Magical African American Friend," a trope that will be explored in full in the chapter that follows. Predictable sidekick roles played by actors like Danny Glover in the *Lethal Weapon* franchise, Ving Rhames in the *Mission: Impossible* movies, and Will Smith in *The Legend of Bagger Vance* have established the trope. All of these roles and narrative forms send the same message of White normality, heroism, and importance, with support offered by Black actors to affirm that White supremacy. This is the telling of stories to appeal to White audiences and leave them feeling affirmed, celebrated, and thought of as normal.

2. POPULAR CULTURE PROMPTS CONVERSATION

Yet in the midst of the problematic and fraught terrain of popular culture, we also suggest that the work done by popular culture production offers one of the most important entryways for education about and resistance to the messages of White supremacy. Whereas many conversations about race get sidelined by the volatility of politically focused discussions, popular culture can offer a place where multiple perspectives meet and find some measure of common cause. A conversation about last night's baseball game can segue into discussion about the many teams who have decided to reject long-standing racist mascots: "Did you hear that the Washington, D.C., football team has decided to 'retire' its racist label? The Cleveland baseball team has followed suit. On the other end, both the Atlanta major-league franchise and the Kansas City NFL team have resisted changing their racist monikers. What do you think about that?" Likewise, a viewing of a movie like *Avatar* opens the possibility of conversations about cultural appropriation. A review of fashion trends allows for examination of the predominance of White models, and engaging with the work of hip-hop artists like Princess Nokia, Childish Gambino, ill Camille, and countless others makes for all kinds of conversations about racial formation in society.

3. POPULAR CULTURE PROVIDES SPIRITUAL ICONS

Popular culture can offer essential artifacts that also can deepen and strengthen our spiritual resources for the struggle against racism. Even while acknowledging concerns about the myth of redemptive violence replete throughout the Marvel universe, we can still find strength and solace in the power, agency, artistry, abundance, and sophistication in the wonderfully Afro-centric images of *Black Panther* (2018). The pages of African American author N. K. Jemisin's Broken Earth trilogy offer images of resilience, alternative understandings of the universe, and Black characters' agency and authority. Kendrick Lamar's "Alright" became an anthem of sorts for #BlackLivesMatter protestors, offering strength and sustenance in the face of both threatened and real violence on the part of counter-protestors and the police.

4. POPULAR CULTURE MODELS RESISTANCE TO RACISM

In the same vein, popular culture artists model how to push back against racism in the media they produce. Where would we be without the lyrical and moving voice of Alice Walker in *The Color Purple*? Her depictions of the resiliency of Black women in the face of sexism and racism continue to resonate, as do her theological insights. At their home in Missoula, Tobin and his wife Cheryl added purple trim to their house to accompany the quote they have hanging on their side fence: "It pisses God off if you walk by the color purple . . . and don't notice it." Walker's character Shug Avery adds, "People think pleasing God is all God cares about. But any fool living in the world can see it always trying to please us back." Shug Avery's words offer a joyful invitation to reorient one's understanding of the nature of the divine in our lives, especially in the midst of resisting racism.

Zora Neale Hurston's *Their Eyes Were Watching God* offers a similar celebration of Black voice and culture even while indicting the racism faced by the community. The title's eponymous quote captures that celebration of Blackness and a countercultural equation with divinity: "They seemed to be staring at the dark, but their eyes were watching God." And the list goes on: Toni Morrison's *Beloved*, Ralph Ellison's *Invisible Man*, Audre Lorde's *Sister Outsider*, bell hooks's *All about Love*, Isabelle Wilkerson's *The Warmth of Other Suns*. The telling of these stories has been showing us how to call out racism in a loud voice, walk toward it without looking away, and naming it in order to end it. That is the power of literature. A good book can indeed change the world.

5. POPULAR CULTURE INVITES CELEBRATION AS SPIRITUAL DISCIPLINE

Those religious communities that have pointed their members to the practice of spiritual discipline through the years do so in order to form and shape the exercise of faith in their daily lives. In this instance, however, rather than suggest one listen to a Queen Latifah or Tracy Chapman album while fasting or watch Spike Lee's *Bamboozled* in the midst of prayer, we note the tradition of celebration as one of the historic spiritual disciplines and point to popular culture as a source of that exercise. The voice of Aretha Franklin, the guitar playing of Jimi Hendrix, the soul of James Brown, the funky beats of Sly and the Family Stone—these are both cause for and means of celebrating in the midst of struggle.

This spiritual discipline of celebration through Black artists' production holds a significant tension for White audiences. One of the few public roles that Black people have been able to claim and maintain in White-dominant space is that of entertainer. In short, White people have long practice at and comfort with being charmed by Black performers. That history has been further complicated by White performers making money by adopting innovations made by Black performers after White critics had dismissed and ridiculed those creative breakthroughs. From White minstrelsy actor Thomas Dartmouth Rice performing in blackface as "Jim Crow" to Elvis Presley copying the blues guitarist Big

Bill Broonzy, the process of cultural appropriation has been ongoing and recurrent.

An antiracist spirituality invites a more grounded and intentional engagement with cultural resources. In workshop settings, we frequently encounter questions about whether wearing clothing from a cultural tradition other than one's own is cultural appropriation or cultural honoring. We usually respond by asking participants to consider whether those who made the clothes for sale are themselves from the identified group, whether appropriate financial payment has been made for community members' labor, and whether that community is being strengthened by others' using their cultural artifacts. The answers to those questions will vary and will lead different individuals to different conclusions. Our point is that shifting away from a discussion of an individual's rights to a consideration of the well-being of the community from which those resources arise is itself a spiritual discipline. With that kind of deliberate honoring, forthright identification, appropriate financial payment, and the acknowledgment of historical traditions, popular culture resources can undergird our celebrations with joy.

6. POPULAR CULTURE THROUGH DRAMA LEADS TO CAREFUL ACTION

Dramatic productions hold particular power to not just educate audiences about racism but move them to action. In the summer of 1996, we helped initiate and administer—along with our colleague Jeannie Romero Talbert—an antiracism drama troupe sponsored by Mennonite Central Committee that traveled up and down the West Coast and eventually came to present at the national Mennonite church convention. Building on the work of Augusto Boal, a Brazilian dramatist and political activist, the team of college-age African American and Latinx young people invited audiences to join the performance by standing up, taking the place of actors, and then trying to bring about alternative endings to real-life scenarios of racism that the young people had encountered in their lives. The actors challenged those who came to their presentations to not just think about racism as an intellectual exercise but also step up, challenge racism where they encountered it, and shake off the strictures of silence and inaction. Members of that troupe have gone on to serve as therapists (Dr. Maribel Hinojosa!), college professors (Dr. Felipe Hinojosa!), early childhood educators (Shyleen Wesley!), and change agents. Their audiences—especially the White people who participated in their reenactments—reported that the presentations stuck with them for months and years. This, too, is antiracism spirituality at work.

7. POPULAR CULTURE LEADS TO LAUGHTER

Popular culture products also make us laugh. But if ever there was an element of an antiracist spirituality that has been underdeveloped and in need of attention, it is humor. Always tricky to navigate, replete with traps, but also filled with healing and hope, the humor of popular culture offers a way to approach racial issues from the side—askance and askew—and in so doing invite audiences to laugh at themselves and learn new insight in the process. The jokester, the trickster, and the comedian poke, startle, sometimes shock, but always invite those listening to revisit the world around them. It is the gift that humor can give us.

Comedian Eddie Murphy starred in a *Saturday Night Live* skit in which he is made up to look like a White man and discovers a previously unencountered world of privilege and access kept hidden from the Black community, including free drinks on bus rides, free money at the bank, and unfettered access to goods and services. He dramatically named the reality of White privilege and lambasted it by exaggerating its effects. Comedian Richard Pryor likewise skewered the racism of the dominant society by speaking without apology about the racism he encountered. In so doing, he cleared a path for others to follow, like Dave Chappelle, Louis C. K., Wanda Sykes, Maya Rudolph, Keegan-Michael Key, and Jordan Peele. Although at times controversial, these comedians loosen racism's grip simply by making fun of it.

Tobin's son Zach once gave a stand-up comedy routine at a local bar in Missoula based entirely on growing up as the son of a White guy who does antiracism work. Zach filled his monologue with bits that skewered Tobin for his at times over-earnest zealotry for the work of dismantling racism. For example, he mocked Tobin's attempt to redeem the association of Blackness with negativity in J. K. Rowling's Harry Potter novels. When reading the books out loud, Tobin would substitute "purple magic" for "black magic." A few years later Zach and his brother then referred to that purple magic when discussing the novels with their middle school peers. Their friends in turn made fun of them. Zach's routine unflinchingly—yet ultimately lovingly—not only critiqued well-meaning White liberals but also called attention to how rare it was for young White males to grow up talking about racism, White privilege, and White supremacy. His roast was just as much a gift as are the ongoing contributions of comedians to racial discourse in this country.

8. POPULAR CULTURE ALSO PROMOTES THE IDEA OF THE WHITE SAVIOR

If we are going to explore the intersections of popular culture and antiracism spirituality in full, we also need to name and pursue how movies in particular present White heroes in the work of dismantling racism. Examples of the so-called "White savior" abound. Sandra Bullock portrays Leigh Anne Tuohy, a White suburban mother who becomes the legal guardian of homeless Black teen football player Michael Oher, in *The Blind Side* (2009), purportedly saving him from impoverishment in the process. In the science fiction film *Avatar* (2009), Sam Worthington plays the part of a White former Marine who helps lead an alien humanoid race—with plenty of Indigenous markers—to victory against colonial forces. Emma Stone plays Eugenia "Skeeter" Phelan in *The Help* (2011) as a White writer who tells the story of Black domestic workers in an effort to address the racism they face in their jobs. These roles and literally dozens more like them repeatedly send the message that Black and Indigenous communities will remain unsuccessful in their struggles to dismantle racism without a White savior figure present to save them and point the way to victory. The producers of *Hidden Figures* (2016) even rewrote the story of the Black female NASA mathematicians who helped calculate flight trajectories in the early years of the U.S. space program. Rather than just focus on the women's contributions and skill in negotiating NASA's racist and sexist policies, the producers created fictional scenes that featured Kevin Costner's White supervisor character pushing back against Jim Crow segregation.

The point is not that White people should refrain from taking action to dismantle racism. Far from it. Rather, it is that these movies cast the White person as the primary agent of change, usually as a lone individual, and so seldom present independent Black action to challenge racism without a White figure leading them to victory. Notable exceptions like *Fruitvale Station* (2013), *Selma* (2014), *I Am Not Your Negro*

(2016), and *Get Out* (2017) counter this trend by placing Black figures as the heroes of their own liberation. An antiracist spirituality not only celebrates and supports this trend but invites White people to join in the antiracist struggle alongside the Black community rather than as the saviors of it.

9. POPULAR CULTURE FOSTERS INTERSECTIONAL DISCUSSION

When we talk and write about racism, we aim to do so in an intersectional manner. We can't talk about racism as if it were isolated and did not connect with how people experience sexism, classism, heterosexism, ableism, and the multiple means of dishing out oppression and privilege in this society. Popular culture products invariably also offer intersecting dimensions in need of attention. If nothing else, they offer a way to exercise and develop the skill of analysis as intersecting oppressions mesh and meld. A film like *Moonlight* (2016) by writer and director Barry Jenkins allows for exploration—among other dynamics—of the interplay of racism and heterosexism. Danny Glover's performance in *To Sleep with Anger* (1990) opens up conversations about class, race, and religion in a Black family in Los Angeles. HBO's *Watchmen* (2019) is a small-screen series based on a graphic novel of the same name that uses superhero allegory to open up opportunities for examining racism and violence in popular culture itself, especially in regards to issues of police abuse.

10. POPULAR CULTURE HELPS US IMAGINE THE FUTURE YET TO BE

Yet analysis of racism can lead to spirit-deadening cynicism. Our longtime colleague Felipe Hinojosa, a history professor at Texas A&M, observes that if all we do is call out and focus on the presence of racism in society without crafting and lifting up alternatives that point to and envision a new way forward, we and the movements in which we are situated will invariably collapse and grind to a halt, victims of our own failure to imagine a new future. Popular culture provides us with a means to also think about what those alternative realities look like, to flesh out their possibility, to enliven and offer hope for a way forward.

As a genre, science fiction's presentation of possible futures has tended toward the dystopian. Think of George Orwell's *1984*, Aldous Huxley's *Brave New World*, or Octavia Butler's *Parable of the Sower*. Movies in the same genre have frequently featured similar dystopian futures—*Snowpiercer* (2013), *District 9* (2009), *Blade Runner* (1982; as well as its 2017 sequel, *Blade Runner 2049*). At root, the narrative presentation of utopian futures that present alternative ways of being in the world can be challenging to an author interested in creating conflict and plot. Yet some have succeeded. Ursula K. Le Guin's work—whether the Earthsea series, her classic novel *The Dispossessed*, or an experimental work of fiction like *Always Coming Home*—offers glimpses of alternative ways of structuring societies. Sheri S. Tepper likewise explored feminist themes in books like *Raising the Stones*. But it has been Black science fictions and speculative fiction authors themselves who have most consistently explored alternative futures and dealt directly with racial themes. Already back in 1859, Black nationalist leader Martin Delany published *Blake*, a novel envisioning a successful revolt of enslaved Africans and their subsequent founding of a new country in Cuba. Since the mid-twentieth century, Black authors like Samuel R. Delany, Nalo Hopkinson, Andrea Hairston, and those we have already highlighted, such as N. K. Jemisin and Octavia Butler, have continued to look ahead, sideways, and back through to declare that the way we are is not the way that we can yet be. Envisioning the future invites us to act differently in the present. Speaking of what might yet come to pass pulls us forward. And that is one of the best things that can come from an antiracist spirituality.

LOVE AND BELOVEDNESS

Throughout this book we have and will continue to tell the story of our separate and intertwined journeys to belovedness. The work we have done individually and as a training, organizing, and writing team to understand ourselves as beloved of God, of our families, of our friends, and of the world around us despite and in the midst of messages that declare Blackness despicable and Whiteness skin-deep has been long-term and required support. It has been spiritual work as much as it has been emotional and psychological. But it has come back time and again to this notion of love.

The culture in which we are situated—both generally and in popular culture terms—speaks much of love. Hypersexualized, made banal, tending toward the saccharine, or spiritualized to the point of disjuncture from the day-to-day, the topic of love is difficult to write about without it becoming either schmaltzy on one end or seductive on the other. Popular culture offers us only glimpses of mature and balanced love of self, of the other, of the enemy. At those points where love is taken as something more than the product of hormones, idealized romance, or the distortion of the male gaze, we gain glimpses of love in its fullest form.

The quirky, mystical, and beautiful film *Beasts of the Southern Wild* (2012) depicts a complex and loving relationship between the young protagonist Hushpuppy (Quvenzhané

Wallis) and her ailing father, Wink (Dwight Henry). The powerful and provocative film version of *Beloved* (1998) offers a moving brush arbor scene in which a female preacher calls for holy self-love as well as a public exorcism of sorts carried out by a collective chorus of Black women come to care for and call back to wholeness the character of Sethe, played by Oprah Winfrey. *Hunt for the Wilderpeople* (2016) shows the flawed but deeply loving relationship between "Uncle" Hector (Sam Neill) and Ricky Baker (Julian Dennison) as they flee a manhunt in the New Zealand bush.[1]

These examples and others like them ultimately turn on bracing honesty, a willingness to stay in relationship despite disappointment, and a commitment to the other's well-being without sacrificing the same for oneself. Those values offer and demonstrate profound spiritual connections. And like all authentic spiritual traditions, the traditions themselves are challenging to maintain. Often, those traditions emerge in the midst of brokenness as much as in the midst of health. Hushpuppy ultimately has to grieve the loss of her father; viewers are left to ponder if they parted after a restored relationship or whether there were elements left unsettled. In *Beloved*, the main character Sethe had killed her daughter in a desperate act to keep her from being re-enslaved. In a turn of magic realism, her daughter than comes back to life and drags Sethe into sickness and delusion. After Sethe is rescued from the embodied reincarnation of her daughter through an exorcism, she falls into a deep depression that begins to be undone only by the return of her suitor Paul D. In *Hunt for the Wilderpeople*, Ricky refuses to abandon Hector even when offered an easy way out from the manhunt that threatens them. Like relationships in real life, the love depicted in these films is messy, hard, and true.

And even discussions about positive interracial relationships in popular culture can be challenging. In preparing for this chapter, we invited Facebook friends to identify healthy relationships captured in film and song. The resulting discussion thread generated more than seventy comments and nearly one hundred specific examples from film, literature, and music. Although not every example was interracial, the ones that were gave us some pause. We noticed that the list generated in our social media accounts included many examples of unequal, superficial, and at times stilted relationships. Our colleague and friend Michelle Armster, the executive director of Mennonite Central Committee Central States and a skilled mediator, wrote, "Many of the examples of 'healthy' interracial relationships are examples of unequal relationship that are based on the forced relationship expected of a person of color to Whiteness. Forced intimacy . . . assumed intimacy . . . and many other issues. My question is: why do those people suggest those movies?!?"

Michelle's question is essential. She referenced examples such as those found in *Driving Miss Daisy* (1989) with a Black chauffer Hoke Colburn (Morgan Freeman) and his White employer Daisy Werthan (Jessica Tandy), Frank "Tony Lip" Vallelonga (Viggo Mortensen) and Dr. Don Shirley (Mahershala Ali) in *Green Book* (2018), Kelly Robinson (Robert Culp) and Alexander "Scotty" Scott (Bill Cosby) in the television series *I Spy* (1965–68). The issue is not that the film and television producers chose to depict Black-White pairs. Rather, it is that the presentation of what those relationships end up entailing is made problematic and unhealthy by the assumptions of the writers and directors who crafted the scripts and framed the relationships.

In fact, of the examples that our social media respondents provided, it is difficult to identify one that is not hampered by the Hollywood tropes that have burdened representations of interracial relationships through the years. In *Be Kind Rewind* (2008), Black actor and hip-hop artist Mos Def ends up being limited by his role as the straight man—Mike Coolwell—to the pranks and mugging of White actor and comedian Jack Black's Jerry Mclean character as the two of them shoot home-made knock-offs of popular movie titles. In *Sister Act* (1992), Whoopi Goldberg plays a Black lounge singer forced into the witness protection program, where she is settled into a convent run by Reverend Mother, played by White actress Maggie Smith, but here again Goldberg's character seldom expands beyond the trope of a Black singer once again performing for the benefit of White audiences. The list, of course, goes on. It is as if the writers of these movies had no models of healthy, mature, non-romantic interracial relationships to draw upon. As if they had never encountered such a connection in real life. Their ability to imagine and portray relationships that cross racial lines but are not ultimately defined by the very kind of unequal and inappropriate dynamics of assumed, forced, and strained intimacy that Michelle identified is limited, if not entirely nonexistent.

To speak of healthy interracial relationships is to raise the prospect of a rare vision, one that we risk corrupting in the very act of describing it. A vision that runs deep in the longing of so many who genuinely desire something better to emerge from our country's racist past and present practice of the same. Martin Luther King called it the beloved community. Others have deemed it a collective of co-strugglers. Sometimes we refer to it simply as the body made whole. We do not mean to thwart the desire for that kind of fully realized reconciliation, but we do caution against fixating on healthy relationships. If we are going to attempt to portray such interracial relationships in a healthy way, an antiracist spirituality calls us not only to have integrity in doing so but to handle that presentation with great and thoughtful care.

Our relationship, while not the stuff of Hollywood films, is at least worthy of comment. To be certain, our friendship is notable to some degree simply because it has lasted three decades. And we have been as honest as we are able to be about the social context in which we have committed ourselves to working together, recognizing the tendencies for both internalized superiority and inferiority to manifest even as we have focused on dismantling them. But naming those realities and tendencies, while important, is not sufficient. We have also invested time—as already noted—in hanging out together with our families, fostering best practices of open communication, principled positioning (i.e., thinking carefully through who speaks first when we co-present), and learning to support and call each other to our best selves.

In short, we have learned to love each other.

In our work with predominantly White institutions interested in dismantling racism, we have learned to speak of and exercise love with great care. A newly promoted regional church executive—a White man—confessed to us that he had tried to limit the authority of the African American pastor of the congregation that he had just left. We expressed our love for him by counseling him to let go of his need for control. In the same way, a White Protestant bishop asked for advice on how best to support a Black pastor of an all-White congregation mired in well-meaning but no less damaging racism. We offered our love to her by suggesting that the bishop help that pastor find a new posting, one where he would not be further traumatized by the congregation's racist practices. We also invited the bishop to reflect on what kept her and her colleagues from stepping in to forestall the assignment from the start, a difficult but necessary conversation. Again, it was an expression of love as best we knew how to offer.

The kind of love that grounds an antiracist spirituality is not just about fondness, care, or tenderness. It is in no way defined by or limited to issues of sexual attraction and romance. As is the case in any spiritual work that invites practitioners to wrestle with the ego, push back against aggrandizement, and nurture authenticity, the work of fostering an antiracist love is not fragile. It does not run on hormones and candy. It is tough and direct and knows no deceit. It does not back down when faced with failure. An antiracist love speaks truth to power. And it prompts laughter, gladness, and a full heart.

We have tried to model that kind of love in our relationship with each other and with those with whom we work. We have done so more successfully at some times than others. When we have glimpsed it, our hearts have been made glad. When we have missed it, well, that is the miracle of having stayed in the struggle. We have then made the decision to stay at it and learn from our errors.

Much more difficult has been our consideration of how best to love the institution most formative on our antiracism work—Mennonite Central Committee. As already evident in our discussion here, we gained much from the platform that MCC offered us in the early years of our work within the Anabaptist community. We would not have been taken as seriously had we not had the MCC imprimatur behind our Damascus Road label. They helped fund and provided the infrastructure for our work for many years. At the same time, the recurrent resistance to unflinchingly acknowledge and directly address the institutional racism in their house has been discouraging. Good friends have been forced out from employment with

MCC because of attempts by those individuals to name racism and hold the institution accountable to address it.

We were even connected to and participated in a campaign to ask constituents to withhold funds after MCC's reorganization plans disproportionately affected People of Color. A daylong mediation meeting offered little in the way of forward movement, even after People of Color on our team again named and identified the racism of the institution. After we had caucused and discussed the perspectives we had shared during the day, a Black woman on our team said, "I simply do not trust them. We have identified at least five different and specific ways that they could restore integrity to their stated antiracism commitments and they have refused them all." The most loving thing we knew to do when we came back together was to tell them that trust had been broken. That we could not, in good faith, continue in the process unless and until action had been taken to ensure that the voices and perspectives of People of Color would not be ignored and dismissed going forward. It is not by accident that no Person of Color has ever held the reins in MCC's highest position of power.

Sometimes the most powerful statement of love one can make is simply to walk away and wish the individual or partner with whom you are in disagreement well but to no longer invest one's energy in the relationship itself. To love from a deep ethic of antiracism can also mean to shut the relationship down.

That kind of story does not play well in Hollywood. It is not a storybook ending. But we know that, particularly for members of the Black, Indigenous, and People of Color communities, it has been necessary at times to do that very thing and walk away. Otherwise, the pace and tenor of White people's process of change ends up defining the relationship, making demands for intimacy and vulnerability on People of Color with little recognition or awareness of those demands. White people in those relationships have too often brought their neediness for affirmation and approval rather than been willing to sit with the discomfort of a racism exposed.

Popular culture will, we think, catch up. Already there are signs of movies and television shows depicting relationships that don't place the White person in the position of authority, that don't just appeal to the White gaze, that don't present casts that are—yet again—diverse only to the point of presenting one, perhaps two, Black or Brown faces in the principal ensemble. The films *Dear White People* (2014), *Get Out* (2017), *Sorry to Bother You* (2018), *Belle* (2013), and *I Am Not Your Negro* (2016) critique contemporary society, push back against the same, and celebrate an alternate reality that is too often ignored in popular culture.

And as that happens, we will be watching, laughing, crying, and learning in the midst of it all.

Chapter 5

Antiracism and Identity

As we've just seen in examples from the previous chapter, popular culture conveys powerful, sustained, pervasive, and often quite subtle messages about racial identity. But they are also changing and becoming more complex. Amid those shifts, one idea with a particular ability to shape racial identities recurs: Black characters should take care of White ones. Take, for example, the 2021 Netflix release of *Lupin*, a mystery/thriller/comedy series, filmed in French with English subtitles starring a Black character, played by Omar Sy, in a long-term relationship with a White woman, played by Ludivine Sagnier, supported by a multiracial cast. All of that is good. But at the same time, the film rarely takes racism head-on, leaves issues of institutional racism largely unaddressed, and makes White audiences feel good by virtue of the interracial friendships portrayed and the fact that the Black hero faces down both White and Black antagonists. The Black caretaker—also referred to by Christopher John Farley as the Magical African American Friend (MAAF) and more problematically in other sources as a "magic Negro"—continues to appear in Hollywood films and streaming media.[1]

The MAAF is a well-established Hollywood trope in which an African American character plays a salvific role in the life of a White person, often through magic or supernatural means, even if it means sacrificing oneself to do so. In the 1958 crime drama *The Defiant Ones*, Sidney Poitier's character sacrifices his chance at freedom to save the life of the White convict played by Tony Curtis. In *The Green Mile* (1999), John Coffey, as played by Michael Clarke Duncan, exercises his healing powers on behalf of a White inmate, White death row guard, and the White wife of the prison warden before being executed. The MAAF trope crops up in a host of other Hollywood dramas, such as with Will Smith in *The Legend of Bagger Vance* (2000), Whoopi Goldberg in *Ghost* (1990), and Morgan Freeman in *The Shawshank Redemption* (1994). The list goes on. The comedy duo Key and Peele spoofed the Hollywood archetype in a hilarious 2012 skit that roasts the trope's reliance on stereotypes.[2]

Of particular importance to the function of a MAAF in these films is that the Black figure—again, most often male but not always; note the Whoopi Goldberg role in *Ghost*—usually comes into the life of the White protagonist from outside. In the case of Will Smith's Bagger Vance, he literally approaches the White lead played by Matt Damon from out of the dark of the night. In few of the films does the Black savior figure stay around in the life of the White person he or she has saved.

WILLIAM PANNELL AND THE MAAF

The case of William E. Pannell, a Black leader from within our own religious community, makes clear how tricky and pervasive the dynamic of the MAAF can be. William E. Pannell came into the White Mennonite community having spent time with Brethren Assemblies in Detroit. By the end of the 1950s, already a well-known evangelist, he began to show up at Mennonite sponsored meetings such as the 1959 roundtable discussion entitled "Program of Witness to and With Negroes," held in Chicago and sponsored by the Home Missions and Evangelism Committee of the Mennonite Church.[3]

Although in these early meetings his voice in the minutes comes across as reconciliatory and appeasing, that would change over time. While in 1959 he commented, "We should remember that our primary problems are the spiritual, and here we must make our basic contributions," a year later in the pages of the Mennonite Church news outlet, the *Gospel Herald*, he caricatured White people as being held hostage by an insurmountable "basic fear" of Black people expressed by trembling "slightly" and mumbling "nonsense about intermarriage."[4] By 1968, an excerpt from his controversial book *My Friend, the Enemy* criticized White-dominated missions conferences sponsored by congregations that relocated from Black neighborhoods even as they claimed to minister to them.[5] As of 1971, he appeared in the pages of the General Conference news magazine, *The Mennonite*, with a reflection on the need for the Black community to have "power, control, the sharing of power."[6] Two years later he also participated in the AFRAM conference held near Nairobi, Kenya, to bring together African American and African Mennonites.[7]

Pannell's Mennonite connections were more extensive than these publications and meetings suggest. He counted White Mennonite church planter Vern Miller as a "friend and brother," even indicating that Miller introduced him to Martin Luther King Jr.[8] He recalled conversations with theologian John Howard Yoder while visiting Goshen College and referenced talks he gave at nearly every Mennonite college and high school as well as to most Black Mennonite congregations in the United States.[9] Even more importantly, Pannell credited Mennonites with forming his "understanding of servanthood, of discipleship, of dimensions of faith in practice," going so far as to exclaim in the course of an oral history interview, "Ah, boy, that was good stuff. I watched them live that stuff out in very uncomfortable circumstances. It helped me enormously."[10]

And the exchange between Pannell and the Mennonite community wasn't just one way. His invitation to participate in the 1973 AFRAM conference was only one indication of the trust that Black Mennonites placed in him. Already in 1968, leaders of the racially integrated Broad Street Mennonite Church in Harrisonburg, Virginia, had invited him to consult with them to discern their role as a church in their immediate neighborhood.[11] White Mennonites also found Pannell's contributions helpful. One reader of The Mennonite praised Pannell for "telling it as it is and honestly facing" racism present within the Mennonite community.[12]

The connection we make between Pannell and the trope of the Magical African American Friend has less to do with the nature of Pannell's specific interactions with both Black and White Mennonites than it does with a larger pattern into which his interactions with Mennonites fit.

Consider the following list: Hubert Brown, Curtis Burrell, Rosemarie Harding, Vincent Harding, Warner Jackson, James Lark, Rowena Lark, Joy Lovett, Stan Maclin, Charles McDowell, Dwight McFadden, John Powell, Ed Riddick. Every one of these high-profile African American individuals appeared on a national Mennonite platform between 1950 and 2000 either as a speaker, author, evangelist, or church official. All of them were initially embraced for the salvific power they brought to the church. All of them at some point found that White Mennonites lost interest once these individuals shifted from helping and affirming to directly challenging the community's racism. Every one of them then left the church for at least a stretch of time or disappeared from national attention.[13] In the case of Pannell, he had never formally joined the Mennonite church.

So this is our question: What does this pattern tell us about antiracism and identity? Each of the individuals listed here is worthy of much fuller attention than what this chapter can offer. The reasons for their specific departures from the Mennonite world range from the most problematic of personal failings to decisions to pursue alternate career paths. But what troubles us as we review this list and ponder the tenure of William Pannell in the Mennonite world is that, like MAAFs, high-profile Black Mennonite leaders have rarely found a long-term home in the church. This pattern among Mennonites has been replicated repeatedly in other predominantly White denominations. Pannell was useful to White Mennonites only for as long as leaders in the community saw him as someone who could help save them. Once he challenged White Mennonites to save themselves and began naming their racism directly, that interest waned.

And, the historical record would suggest, there is a through line in the personal narratives behind these names that speaks of White members of religious communities being willing to be challenged for a period of time but only, in the words of Pannell, in "relationship to a suitcase." Here is what Pannell wrote back in 1968. His words are worth quoting in full:

> It took considerable time, several years in fact, before I began to realize that there were any number of people whose acceptance of me was conditioned by my relationship to a suitcase. A singing Negro has always been welcome as

long as he is a vagabond, and has no intention to settle
with his family. Again this is an overstatement since many
would have been delighted if I would have stayed. But they
too disappoint me when I discover their unwillingness to
fight for my right to stay against those entrenched local
forces of bigotry. They handcuffed me to my suitcase by
their silence.[14]

Pannell wrote these words now more than fifty years ago.
The Mennonite community today counts a host of Black
leaders who have stayed and are leading the church: Michelle
Armster, Leslie Francisco III, Stanley Green, Glen Guyton,
Cyneatha Millsaps, and, of course, Regina Shands Stoltzfus.
Yet even these leaders have mentioned the discomfort they
regularly encounter as they have worked to establish themselves as fully belonging to the church community, as being
something much more than is defined by a suitcase waiting at
the church's back door.

In our work together, we, too, have had to guard against the
MAAF trope. We have actively refused to allow Regina to be
placed in the helper/salvific/guru role, as if only there to assist
Tobin on his way. We have paid attention to how we relate to
each other so as not to replicate a pattern where the White
man draws on the Black woman's strength to persevere. At the
same time, we are friends and do discuss the challenges that
we both face.

One of the reasons our writing and training partnership
has worked for as long as it has is that we have a pretty good
sense of who we are both in terms of our racial identities and
in terms of our sense of belovedness. Regina has long been
grounded in her identity as a Black woman. She was socialized into Black racial consciousness in large part because of
where and when she grew up—in a segregated city during

the 1960s and '70s. Her parents, who met in Cleveland, both migrated from the South for better job opportunities. News about racial unrest across the country and the civil rights movement happened against the backdrop of daily life. That period also encompassed the Black Power movement, which made messages about Black beauty and pride also ever present. Her parents, children, and extended family—both fictive and blood-defined—remind her that she is much loved and treasured on a daily basis.

It has taken Tobin longer to be comfortable in his skin as a White man. So much in our culture keeps White identity unnamed and invisible or only uncomfortably addressed. But for at least the last two decades, he has learned to name and love himself as a White man. His family—again, both fictive and blood-defined—likewise reminds him that he, too, is much loved and treasured on a daily basis.

But from that bedrock foundation of belovedness our respective issues of identity diverge. Regina lives in a country that has from its inception been ingrained with and defined by both anti-Blackness and White supremacy. She has regularly received messages that she and those who look like her are less than, inferior, and insufficient for the tasks of living. Tobin lives in that same country but has received messages that he and those who look like him are more than, superior, and more than capable of meeting the tasks of living. That identity is further amplified and supported by a parallel set of messages about the superiority of men and those in the middle and upper classes, as well as those who are able-bodied, heterosexual, and cisgender.

Relationships are always complex. But a principled and informed intentionality helps us negotiate the many traps integrated (pun entirely intended) into the fabric of our friendship.

FOUNDATIONAL PRACTICES FOR INTEGRATED
RELATIONSHIPS

We have invested significant time and attention in exploring identity issues that have emerged separately within White and People of Color communities. That work does take particular and specific attention. Yet we support and recognize the importance of doing that separate work and then finding ways to come back together to work alongside and in collaboration with each other.

It is perhaps an expected turn at the end of a discussion of antiracism and identity to celebrate and affirm the rightness of a racially integrated approach, of the value of integration, of the beloved community. To be certain, we do value all of those things. We would not have spent thirty years collaborating together if we did not.

But concurrent with that affirmation, we also recognize how the easy and quick affirmation of and support for discussions of integration across racial lines can do as much damage as repair. Integration without restitution and reparation is cheap. It ends up silencing the voice of prophecy, chiding those who speak to ongoing issues of inequity, presenting criticism as burden rather than gift. It is the first move of White institutions. It is the demand for grace when the ongoing reality of racial oppression has not abated.

An antiracist spirituality that has integrity in working across racial lines of distinct racial identities is in the end marked by three foundational practices. We offer them cautiously, in light of the caveats that we have thus far named, with a request that they not be presented as a quick and easy way to jump to any notion of reconciliation without engaging the more difficult work of restoration.

The first is a practice that has received less attention among those working in the field of antiracism: the heart and gut work of grieving on both the individual and collective levels. The White community in particular has largely been silent and removed from any process of grieving for our participation in racism, our benefit from that participation, our acceptance of the legacy of that benefit, and our loss of vibrant cultural identities because of the creation of a White collective identity.

For White people, the work of grieving in order to enter into sustained and healthy partnerships across racial lines is not simply an act of saying "I'm sorry." On an individual level, it is at minimum to acknowledge the deep pain present in this country from the past exercise of racism and the ongoing practice of the same. Even if, as is the case for so many White people and especially White men, only numbness exists where that pain might be felt, sitting with the knowledge of that pain in the course of personal devotion, meditation, or prayer can be one way to move toward an actual experience of that grief.

On a collective level, the White community has work to do in our respective communities to ritualize that grief process. Every religious tradition has some means of naming and processing its grief. How those rituals and services might be molded and shaped to lead communities through such a process of grief is a task for religious leaders that calls on the best of both the pastoral and prophetic traditions. One predominantly White congregation in the Pacific Northwest developed a ritual to mark the beginning of a process that would bring them to reckon with the practices of institutional racism in their church community. It included a liturgy, a prayer, and a time of silent grieving.

Such a process of grieving is not, of course, once and done. It is rarely clean and straightforward. It can involve emotional messiness, expression of deep hurt, going forward, and shifting back. The scale will be one of years, not weeks or days.

Grief is not easily finished. It does take time.

We start by naming the importance of grief in developing sustainable relationships across racial lines because to skip over that grief invariably leads to immature, surface-level, and unsustainable relationships. In a context in which so many of the wounds of racism lie gaping all around, to fail to grieve is to shut down one's ability to connect, to be honest, to embody truth in one's relationship where that reality will always be a live backdrop. Grief opens the door to authenticity.

The second grounding practice is a commitment to give veto power to the Persons of Color in the partnership. What we mean—and what we have practiced in our work together these many years—is a conscious, clear, and sustained practice that if we cannot agree on a path forward about a given decision, Regina has veto power. While we have seldom had to enact that principle, our commitment to it has been a concrete and palpable way of acknowledging the powerful forces of racism and sexism arrayed in our society that continue to direct power and privilege in Tobin's direction and shift them away from Regina. The articulation of and commitment to that principle does not end those systems of racism and sexism, but it does set an anchor that provides a measure of mooring against them.

People make assumptions about being friends. We have often encountered the assumption that our partnership just sort of happened. That it didn't take work, trust, or a veto principle to ground it. That there weren't plenty of setbacks along the way. The principle of veto power is no substitute for doing the work together, building the trust, risking enough to both make and learn from mistakes. Yet that principle and its practice have guided us through some challenging decisions and painful conflicts.

We continue to practice it.

That said, we are also aware that we haven't thought about it for a long time. As we talked about and prepared for writing this section, we realized that the more we have lived out that principle, the less we have had to verbally articulate it because we have internalized it. The principle itself has become a trusted mentor to our work together. It takes a long time—to be certain. But the practice has been an essential component of our work together. Without it, we are fairly certain we would not have kept working together, particularly in the early stages of our partnership. We certainly would not have been able to counter the temptation to slip into the roles suggested by the trope of the Magical African American Friend and the White people the MAAF ends up serving.

The third practice is best stated by saying that we are about more than just the work. In the early years of our work with Damascus Road, we would bring together our training team and our accountability group for work sessions. Very early on, we made the decision that our time together would not just be invested in labor. Our sponsoring institution supported a work ethic that left little time for enjoying each other's company. If money was to be spent on bringing people together for meetings, then meet they would. Long days and even longer nights spent in meeting after meeting was the order of the day. We said, "That's not how we are going to be. We are more than just the work."

So we structured our time as a training and leadership team to be as much about building authentic relationships as about making decisions. In short, we made sure that we hung out together. We invested our time in singing together, joking with each other, praying together, and going out to eat together. Both of us hold and cherish memories of the many, many times that we sat around a table over good food and drink and laughed and were truly present with our team. Our children even talk about the social events that we held together as highlights of their childhood when living rooms or church fellowship halls would be filled with all God's children—whom they knew by name and who knew their names in return—gathered together because there was a common struggle and a common recognition of the power of connection in the midst of the work against racism.

Regina regularly reminds the young, passionate, and focused students who throng to her classes that the work does indeed require more than just the work. She says to them, "If there is not joy in it, you're not going to keep doing it."

For the months that we were focused on the composition of this book, we met by Zoom every Monday at 2:30 p.m. EST/12:30 p.m. MST (time zones have become more of a challenge for us as we have aged and lived across two of them—we have learned to always spell them out). Some of our time would be spent talking through compositional issues, editing challenges, and the ongoing work of crafting a unified voice. But we also just hung out. We told stories of the week—invariably filled for both of us with conversations and discussions of racism through our teaching and consulting work—and chatted about cultural events and invariably gossiped a bit about people that we know in common. Regina can rarely resist the opportunity to tease Tobin about his CrossFit-style workouts or what she describes as the antiracism training "empire" that has emerged around the work of Widerstand Consulting.

Tobin does his best to mirror the repartee but long ago recognized—as his sons have pointed out—that when he tries to be funny he just ends up sounding mean. But the point is that we probably spend at least as much time just chatting about the stuff of life as we do about the work before us. Even so, the rhythm of that work cycle also has made evident that we get through the work itself far more quickly because we spend the time investing in our relationship and simply building joy.

Our identities are powerful. When we work together across racial lines, we bring the brokenness as well as the promise of repair. An antiracist spirituality that opens space for grieving, is grounded by the veto power principle, and fosters relationship by nurturing joy—that is a gift. One that we acknowledge we have not brought about just by our efforts but has simply been present, a gift, which we cherish and stand amazed that it has endured. We remain grateful for this opportunity to share a modicum of insight about how it might be nurtured elsewhere as well.

Chapter 6

Responding to Whiteness

Part of a principled and informed antiracist spirituality includes investing time and attention into how racism has shaped our respective racial identities. For Tobin, this has meant an ever deeper awareness of the paradoxical harm done by racism to White people.[1] To address this topic, he here tells the story of a night when he discovered something about himself in particular, White people in general, and the movement of the Spirit in regards to the same.

CALLING TO REFLECTION ON WHITE IDENTITY

The Episcopalians who logged in for a virtual discussion of faith and race on a cold night in early December welcomed me warmly. Some of them I knew from the short-lived dalliance Cheryl and I had with their congregation's choir before COVID hit Montana in the spring of 2020. Others had taken non-credit classes with me. So I recognized many of their faces on the screen.

When one of the congregation's priests had approached me about speaking, I proposed a discussion focusing on White identity and spiritual formation. It seemed like a safe topic, one that would not require a great deal of emotional investment on my part.

I had spoken about similar themes many times.

About five minutes before we were set to begin, however, I felt prompted to change my opening. Rather than pose an academic question, I felt nudged to talk about a personal struggle I'd been facing.

But I did not want to do so.

After Cheryl and I founded a new nonprofit, Widerstand Consulting, to reinvest the speaking and consulting funds I had earned in the aftermath of George Floyd's murder in the summer and fall of 2020, I had begun to recognize that I resented giving the money away. The nonprofit covered our operating expenses, to be sure. But I still found myself resentful of the thousands of dollars we gave away. Not all of me. But part of me really wanted to keep that cash.

I had discussed it with Cheryl and she reminded me that we had enough. We did not need that extra. We both wanted to reinvest it in People of Color–led racial justice groups.

I was grateful to be able to do so.

But nonetheless the resentment was there.

So, perhaps against my better judgment, I started my talk to this group of Montanan Episcopalians by telling them of my struggle and asking whether there might be—as I strongly suspected—some connection between that feeling of resentment and my spiritual formation as a White person.

I then did my best to fumble through an explanation of how I connected the dots between that feeling of reluctance/resentment and my White identity.

I started with a history of Whiteness. I told the group that in the process of becoming White, members of specific European groups—the Irish, the English, Italians, and so on—gave up some of their own culturally rooted traditions for access to power and privilege. Historians like Noel Ignatiev, David Roediger, and others have filled in that story with rich detail and analysis. They have noted how the watering down of that cultural identity to the occasional holiday or cultural celebration—think Saint Patrick's Day for the Irish—was necessary for full inclusion in the White community because the entire point of being White was to not have to name one's racial identity in order for White supremacy to remain intact. The less a group drew attention to the remnants of their ethnic and cultural heritage, the more they added to the White majority, the better they acquiesced to notions of White supremacy, the harder it became to distinguish them from any other so-called White person.

I then talked about how that historical process of White identity development set up a damaging dynamic for the White community. I described how jettisoning specific cultural practices created a cultural vacuum that White people have often sought over time to fill by appropriating the cultural traditions of other groups. Those who no longer turned to their own cultural background for sustenance, strength, and support turned elsewhere or did not turn at all. Traditions of dance, dress, music, art, and story thinned, waned, and in some cases sputtered out entirely. The example of German lederhosen make the point. The leather knee-length breeches have become objects of ridicule and humor when worn in all but the most specific of circumstances (such as during Oktoberfest), while tremendous cachet has often gone to those who wear the traditional garb of international or Indigenous groups to which they do not belong.

I then suggested to the group that this kind of cultural vacuum has had spiritual consequences. One of them is that in the absence of those spiritually grounded cultural traditions, White people have often come to rely more on racism's provision of privilege and power than on the providence afforded by spiritual means. Both a psychological and spiritual shift, the dynamic is best described as a reorientation or expectation. Rather than turning toward and becoming grounded in a given community's spiritual traditions, over time those who had come to be called White grew more and more separated from those spiritual traditions and increasingly dependent on a system that called them better than the communities of color around them.

Black sociologist and historian W. E. B. Du Bois described it this way: "It must be remembered that the white group of laborers, while they received a low wage, were compensated in part by a sort of public and psychological wage. They were given public deference and titles of courtesy because they were white."[2] What was true among lower-class White people was only further amplified among the middle and upper classes. Across class lines, White people received a psychological wage of Whiteness—to echo both Du Bois's phrase and that of historian David Roediger. White people had come to claim both the psychological benefit of asserting their group's superiority and the material benefit of oppressing other groups for capital gain. The psychological and material benefits amplified and intensified membership in the White community.

I then turned to the most important point I wanted to make about the negative effects of Whiteness. If the systems of racism around you provide you with unearned advantage and benefit at the expense of People of Color, it simply becomes less necessary to think about, rely on, or be nurtured by one's spiritual traditions and community. What is not exercised, diminishes. What one does not call upon, becomes strange. Past practices are lost. The very thought of spiritual support for life's challenges is disconnected from history and tradition. In the process, spiritual practices become ethereal and separated from real-life struggle, pointing toward eternal reward in the afterlife rather than connection to struggles in the present.

I then made the connection to my feelings about giving away my consulting fees. I wondered with this group of Episcopalians if part of my spiritual formation as a White person had conditioned me to rely more on money and the security it offered than on God's providence. I did not suggest that earning funds and being paid for demanding labor was in any way inappropriate. I did wonder whether the historical processes I had just described had resulted at least in part in an internal space where I resented giving away the money we were bringing in through Widerstand's speaking and consulting contracts. Rather than gracious gratitude, I was left with shriveled resentment.

As I said, I would have rather not discussed this connection. It felt tawdry, shallow, spindly, and brittle all at the same time. It was not in keeping with the "he has it together White anti-racist professional" persona that I wanted to project.

But the questions that then came spilling out seemed to suggest a different outcome. Rather than being put off by my comments, people were drawn in.

They asked me what else I thought might be the reason for my resentment. (I replied, "I am conditioned to see my worth in *what I earn* far more than in *who I am*.")

They wanted to know whether this dynamic was also present among those White evangelicals who supported President Trump despite his White nationalist and openly misogynistic actions. (I said, "Yes. It comes replete with the additional baggage of seeing in the Trump administration a fulfillment of biblical prophecy, but the underlying dynamic remains the same.")

And they asked whether I was suggesting that some traditions of spiritual formation were superior to others. (I commented, "No, but any tradition that has not taken racialization into account is hampered by a significant blind spot in its thinking.")

It was a rich conversation.

But the clearest memory I have of the evening's exchange was with an older member of the congregation. He gazed out at me from the computer screen and said, "Tobin, I'm not sure if I believe everything that you said, but because you made yourself vulnerable tonight, I'm going to think a lot more about this." There was no rancor in his voice. He did not sound distressed. He was curious, even perhaps intrigued. I am confident that he did, indeed, continue to consider how racism might have come to shape who he was and how he experienced his faith.

THE EFFECTS OF RACISM ON WHITE PEOPLE'S SPIRITUALITY

The story that Tobin tells here from his exploration of culture and identity reflects a larger trend that we have noticed in many other settings as well. White tourists flock to Black

Baptist church services in places like Harlem to soak up and participate in the robust spiritual traditions practiced there. New Age practitioners attempt to replicate Native American spiritual practices without connection to or accountability with Indigenous communities. Those seeking financial gain from others' spiritual practices market "sage smudge kits," thereby divorcing the practices of Native communities from the times, places, and peoples in which they are situated.

Racism has had real effects on White people's spiritual practices and collective identity. Those negative effects are no less real and palpable for often remaining unexamined and unacknowledged within White religious communities. This, of course, is not to say that there are no White individuals who have grown spiritually or that all members of the Black or Indigenous communities are spiritual giants. It is to note, however, that these trends have remained consistent, widespread, and well developed over time and across regions of North America. Nothing more but, also and certainly, nothing less.

The next question that usually arises from White participants in workshops that we lead when we focus on the effects of White racial identity is, "So what are White people supposed to then do? Are we supposed to become more White? Stop being White? Neither seems quite right."

Our response is most often that White people need to start by spending some time talking about being White. White caucusing is one way to make that happen. Tobin again speaks from his experience working with and leading White caucuses to explore this first step in addressing White identity:[3]

I remember my first White caucus. I felt a palpable tension as I sat down. When would the yelling start? I was quite frightened about the possibility of being verbally attacked or having to sit and watch other White people excoriate other

White people. I had seen that dynamic unfold in politically progressive circles more times than I wanted to.

If there wasn't going to be that kind of discord, if this was a politer crowd, what would we talk about? How would we spend a full hour focusing on racism without having any People of Color present? Whenever I had talked about racism in the past, there had always been Black or Brown folk around to keep things moving and guide our conversation. I simply could not imagine what an evening's conversation with White people entirely focused on the topic of racism could look like. It seemed very dangerous to me.

Yes, by evening's end there had been no rancor, and I left thinking about all I had learned. We had even laughed at times—at ourselves mostly but also at the world around us. At no point had we focused our attention on talking about the People of Color with whom we worked. That was not the point of the conversation. Far from it. We were there to talk about our role in perpetuating and maintaining a racist society.

So why had I felt so uncomfortable before we met? What was the source of my trepidation? Why had it taken such a big push to get me out the door and to the White caucus?

After giving it more reflection, I arrived at a simple conclusion. My discomfort stemmed from a basic fact: White people have little interest in or experience with talking to other White people about being White people. Even though many of us live, work, and worship in predominantly—if not exclusively—White communities, rarely do we turn the attention of those communities to the very large and very White elephant in the room. That remains as true now as it was thirty years ago when I attended my first White caucus.

And yet White caucusing remains a powerful tool. It offers White people a means to deal with the ways White privilege fosters microaggressions, White fragility, and overt aggression. It allows for exploring questions and working through issues without requiring that People of Color sit through our struggles to come to terms with our racial identity. White caucusing opens space for practicing how to respond to racist comments, reach those consciously or subconsciously invested in White supremacy, and find a spiritual path forward that is authentic to our experience without relying on the spiritual traditions of Black, Brown, or Indigenous communities to provide that for us. And perhaps most importantly, we who are White can build community through White caucusing through which we can support each other to act in new, antiracist ways.

Of course, White caucuses do not have to be only a formally organized group, though such groups can be helpful. White caucuses can take many forms as well. Some of the most powerful White caucuses in which I have participated have been conversations with only one or two other White people. In the late 1980s, I was working for Mennonite Central Committee in New Orleans. One of my mentors, Rev. David Billings, a White Methodist minister, stood with me on a street corner in an African American neighborhood and asked, "What do people see when they look at you?" I answered, "A well-meaning person who has come to help end injustice in this community." Without missing a beat, David replied, "Nope. They see a White guy." I responded, somewhat defensively I might add, "But I'm a Mennonite. I don't even think of myself as a White person." David told me, "It really doesn't matter how you think about yourself. What people see and what society responds to is a White man. You need to be aware of that. And you need to figure out what being White has done to you." That informal White caucus was formative and provocative. It set me on a path that in some ways led to me writing this book with Regina. I am grateful for the honesty and insight that Rev. Billings offered me that day.

Since that time, I've been in dozens of meeting rooms, coffee shops, and virtual spaces talking with other White people about what being White means for our involvement in social justice struggles and how it affects our sense of self and identity. Out of those many formal and informal conversations a few consistent themes have emerged that I'll share here.

HOW TO HOLD A WHITE CAUCUS WITH INTEGRITY

First, White caucusing can be joyful, but it takes a bit of work to get there. To be certain, it can be challenging to discuss blindness to our privilege, reluctance to believe People of Color, or difficulty in taking leadership from People of Color. All these are areas for reflection, response, and principled action. But when we squarely address them, it is also possible to find joy in the work together. I continue to be grateful for Lorraine Stutzman Amstutz, Phil Morice Brubaker, Rick Derksen, Brenda Zook Friesen, and so many other White folks who have challenged, helped form, and held me accountable over these many years. We have learned to laugh together while doing so. At times, the initial conversations have been a bit awkward, but where we end up is worth the investment of time to get there.

But how we set up and participate in White caucusing is as essential to consider as the end result of those efforts. In short, White caucusing needs to be principled and accountable. A White caucus is not a chance for White people to sit around and gripe about People of Color. It is not a time for us as White people to figure out how to avoid struggling alongside communities of color. It is a time to focus on equipping ourselves to do the work of dismantling racism. That does not mean that these meetings are designed to be an opportunity to beat each other up, to go through some kind of critical consciousness therapy where the point is to make each other feel as awful as possible in order to have said that we went through a process of feeling as awful as possible and therefore don't have to ever go through that kind of process again. Rather, the principles of White caucusing—of remaining focused on our experience, of recognizing that the work of White caucusing is to support each other to act in more principled and courageous ways rather than back away from or detract from such risk-taking—can guide us to effective and sustainable action.

Those conversations, of course, need to be nuanced and make connections with the full breadth of our being. We are never only defined by our racial identities. At the same time, there is great promise and danger in intersectionality. This gift of the womanist movement reminds us that we are never just one identity. We are many. As White people caucus, we need to make connections with questions of class, gender, sexual orientation, physical ability, age, and body image because they all affect how we experience the dynamics of White privilege. At the same time, I have observed repeatedly that White folks often use the idea of intersectionality to shift attention away from discussions of race and Whiteness. Most consistently within White groups, a conversational turn toward intersectionality usually leaves racism behind. In the context of White caucuses, intersectionality needs to deepen our analysis of Whiteness, not detract from it.

I've also recognized within myself and noticed in groups of which I've been a part that White caucusing can sometimes be a time when White people end up flashing their "wokeness" badges. That is, they try to prove just how accomplished they are in their White allyship, how brilliant their antiracism organizing, how sustained their work at dismantling institutional racism. But White caucusing is not a time to flaunt our "wokeness." It is a time to honestly share about our successes and our failings—and to support those who find themselves in the midst of real-life struggles.

But even though it is essential and offers great potential for growth and development—particularly when approached as an exercise in spiritual development—White caucusing is not the end goal. The White caucusing process is a way to come apart in order to come back together. When we have invested in White caucuses, our work in racially integrated settings becomes more effective, demands less of the People of Color around us, and lays the foundation for the actual dismantling of racism in our society. I continue to believe in and hold up the image of the beloved community in which all people are working, worshiping, and serving together. But we can't claim that vision until we have refused to replicate the colonialist, imperialist, and White supremacist patterns that are so often part of well-meaning, well-intentioned White liberals' engagement in racially integrated settings.

REACHING OUT TO OTHER WHITE PEOPLE

The topic of antiracism and identity calls for additional attention to the specific strategies and means of reaching out to connect with White people who would just rather not discuss the topic at all. Given how often such conversations end up breaking down into shouting matches, boiling over, damaging relationships, and hardening positions rather than softening them, the topic deserves its own attention. Both of us have invested a great deal of time and energy across the thirty years of our collaboration talking with White people about racism and White supremacy. Over time, we've noticed a few things about how we engage with other White people that have been most effective and have, at the very least, led to longer and more sustained conversations.

For example, we have stopped trying to convince people of anything. This sounds disingenuous at first blush. We are, after all, writing a book and as such are engaged in a rhetorical project that is, at root, attempting to convince others about the importance of an antiracist spirituality. But the assertion remains true. We have learned that it works far better to focus on making sure that the information and ideas we have to share about racism and White supremacy are understandable. If they can be understood, they hold their own power and salience. We leave much more to the ideas and the knowledge on which they are based to do their own work. They do not need us to do it for them. When we have tried to coerce others into thinking as we have, it has invariably been counterproductive.

We have also learned to draw attention to the racially specific ways that White people and People of Color talk about racism and White supremacy. Light bulbs often go off when White people realize that most conversations in the White community about racism (if they happen at all) are focused on interpersonal dynamics. Pointing out that People of Color most consistently discuss racism from a systemic perspective can open the way to a conversation about what systemic racism is. We note that these are large and consistent patterns of conduct. Exceptions remain, but the patterns have, unfortunately, held true across time and space.

We've also come to believe that guilt-tripping is ineffective. We've never really been successful at trying to get White people to change their beliefs by making them feel guilty about being

White. It just doesn't have a very good track record. Although guilt can be effective to motivate individuals who have engaged specifically in overt acts of racism for which there needs to be restitution, having guilt for a received identity is rarely helpful. The question is not how we can make White people feel guilty for being White. The question is how we can support White people to acknowledge that identity and act in new ways that move through that identity rather than reject it.

We also recognize that it can be very threatening for White people to come to grips with their involvement in White supremacy. Tobin remembers how threatened he felt the first time someone challenged him about his involvement in White supremacy. Given that not having to think about being White is the fundamental White privilege (or so we argue), being asked to think about it in a focused manner is not only unfamiliar to most White people; it is highly threatening. It shouldn't be that way, but it is. Too often. In too many different settings. Acknowledging that reality can help evoke a mature compassion both uncompromising and focused on drawing individuals to the possibility of action and new purpose.

Alongside that embrace of compassion, we have learned to focus on the principle of integrity. When speaking to members of faith communities, we talk about how our witness and mission are severely undermined by the racist systems that serve us. We note how racism gets in the way of fulfilling our mission and mandate in the world. Thus, one motivation for doing the work of dismantling racism—regardless of how uncomfortable it may make us—is that by doing so we are restored to integrity. When speaking with those who care about the republic—that is to those who claim the foundational notions that we have claimed as central to the United States' foundation—we note that racism also undermines our traditions of democracy. In one workshop, an angry White man became a respectful and far more engaged participant after a brief exchange about and reminder of those values. Likewise, those who value honesty and integrity more generally also have been willing to talk about how the receipt of White privilege falsifies and distorts their self-perception and way of moving through the world. Again, racism erodes integrity. An antiracist spirituality helps restore it.

We also try to be honest and transparent about our own struggles. While we have to be careful not to end up being precious or condescending, it does us no good to present ourselves as having all the answers. We acknowledge that we both spent time early in our careers extolling the virtues of "prejudice reduction," with no awareness at the time of just how problematic that concept is in terms of suggesting that it is enough to reduce one's prejudices, that the problem of racism is limited to the matter of individual perception—not to mention the problem with how rarely the term *racism* gets used in that approach. Tobin has learned to reflect on times when he has remained silent when he should have spoken up, on his own use of racist stereotypes in casual speech, and on his struggles with accepting leadership from People of Color.

In conversations with White people about racism, we likewise affirm whatever we can. If we notice a kernel of awareness, we ferret it out and acknowledge it. For example, in another workshop setting, a White woman reflected on her background growing up in the South and that she had been unaware of the history of racism within the United States, let alone that same history within her religious community. She posited that she had generally remained innocent of much of the same since that time. Rather than criticize her for that lack of awareness, we invited her to reflect on what that lack of awareness had cost her through the years. Again, we have had to learn not to do so in a condescending manner.

Those conversations have led us to recognize that human connection is important *and* that conflict is okay. Despite our familiarity with and, in Regina's case, expertise in conflict transformation and mediation, we recognize that we both prefer to avoid conflict when possible. We know that all the research makes evident that conflict is natural, normal, and neutral—if not essential. Tobin acknowledges that in the past, in the midst of conflict, his impulse has often been to disparage the other White person. Occasionally he has been able to ground himself and enter conflict without becoming anxious. Many times he has failed at doing so. For both of us, the ongoing challenge has been to figure out how to remain connected to those with whom we are in conflict around issues of racism without betraying either our commitments to antiracism or our relationships.

Tobin has maintained a long-term relationship with a former student—a White male lawyer—who describes himself as politically conservative. Even though the two of them don't arrive at the same political positions, they have remained connected and opened up respectful lines of communication as they have continued to discuss the nature and presence of institutional, cultural, and systemic racism. In fact, this student invited Tobin to officiate at his wedding, and Tobin did so gladly.

Finally, both of us have worked hard to become familiar and comfortable with the language of institutions and systems and have examples at the ready. Again, our goal has not been to convince others about their involvement in racism and White supremacy. But the more we can help others understand, for example, the racism present in real estate practices, the criminal justice system, and the healthcare system—to use just three such examples—the more it becomes possible that those we are speaking with may reconsider how racism operates around them.

Chapter 7

Antiracism and the Spirituality of Conflict and Crisis

THE CRISIS EMBEDDED IN RACISM

Everything was fine until you started stirring things up." We get this a lot. It's pretty common to see some version of this statement in the comments section of news articles dealing with race. It's often paired with a question: "Why do you have to drag race into everything?" Two things are at work here: anxiety about conflict, and ignorance about the pervasiveness of race—how it is built into our structures and orchestrates our lives. When race constrains the lives of People of Color, they feel and see it. When race benefits White people's lives, it's credited to the myth of meritocracy and not a system that advantages some and disadvantages others. In the latter part of the twentieth century, the melting pot myth and the pursuit of colorblindness as a way of fixing race problems have made the ability to understand racial dynamics even more difficult.

To a degree, the practice of conflict transformation can be useful in thinking about crises caused by the inability to understand race, the purposes racialization serves, and racism. (Before reading on, a caution: this is not to say that conflict transformation skills are the key to ending racism. On the contrary, this has been a tool often poorly and inappropriately used in circumstances where systemic oppression is a factor.) I (Regina) teach mediation, and we do a lot of role-plays. They are a critical part of the learning experience, but it often takes people a while to warm up to the idea of doing them. The performance aspect is nerve-racking for sure, especially for introverts or people who don't consider themselves "performers." It's a kind of public speaking, which frightens lots of people. Some people *love* role-plays, but they tend to be in the minority. Nevertheless, the practice is necessary because mediators need to "feel" the role in their bodies, and to develop their own style of working with diverse circumstances, communication styles, and problems.

But students or workshop participants sometimes complain that they can't "get into" the conflicts of the fictional parties— the issues were things they personally would not get upset about. Because students do not have empathy for the fictional parties, they are unable to live into the role-play. Mediators don't need to have the same responses to events as their parties. However, they must have empathy for their parties. Even if they would not get upset or angry about the same thing happening to them, they need to acknowledge and even respect where the parties in conflict are coming from; otherwise, they will be ineffective as mediators.

A lack of empathy plays a significant role in racialized conflicts, and this lack of empathy is a direct result of how race
has functioned. Race relations along the Black/White binary
developed under the laws of subjugation and segregation. By
law and by custom, we were kept from knowing one another.
Most White people have not even had to think about people
who are not White in their day-to-day goings-on. People of
Color are invisible, except when we are hyper-visible.

Our legacy of segregation has created a perfect setting for
this absence of empathy, for how can you be empathetic toward
someone you cannot even imagine at best, or about whom
you've been fed a steady diet of information about who "they"
are? Degrees of this kind of unknowing exist on either side of
the racial divide, but they also operate within an imbalance
of power. For one side, the not knowing is inconsequential;
for the other, it can be deadly. We often use this quote from
longtime antiracism educator and organizer Robert Terry in
our work: "Being white means not having to think about it."
Yet Black people must learn "the ways of white folks" in order
to be safe.

Historically, Whiteness happened to people who had previously identified themselves as part of an ethnic group or a
nation. But in the U.S. system of race, Whiteness became a way
of ranking; some had it bestowed on them, while others had to
earn it. But it always came with the benefit of not being Black,
Brown, or Indigenous. Being White meant being able to own
land and other property. These resources, the building blocks
of wealth, came as a direct result of policies and practices that
caused the continual decimation of Indigenous people's identity, place, and resources, and cut off Black people's ownership
of their own bodies.

Historian Nell Irwin Painter illustrates how this socialization has been necessary since the time of slavery in order to continue to compel White people to participate in this system.

John Nelson was a Virginian who spoke in 1839 about his own coming of age and this system of triangles. He says, when he was a child, when his father beat their slaves, that he would cry and he would feel for the slave who was being inflicted with violence. He would feel almost as if he himself were being beaten, and he would cry. And he would say, "Stop, stop!" And his father [would say], "You have to stop that. You have to learn to do this, yourself." And as John Nelson grew up, he did learn how to do it. And he said in 1839 that he got to the point where he not only didn't cry; he could inflict a beating himself and not even feel it.[1]

Painter calls slavery-induced trauma "soul murder," a phenomenon with deep psychological impact that has created a culture based on domination and ownership:

Within this plantation household, little kids would be learning lessons. . . . So a white child would learn lessons, as well as black children. A white child seeing the violence that goes on between owners and slaves learns: "Well, I can do that. I have power too." And I've read many an anecdote from slaves and from slaveowning families about the point where the white child no longer plays with the black children as an equal, but begins to give them orders—around 5, 6, 7 . . . the white child learns that he can give orders. . . . But the great lesson is that I (child) can inflict violence, can give orders, must be obeyed, and I am someone to whom others owe submission.[2]

These "lessons" did not end with slavery but were reinscribed generation after generation. The family is a site of identity formation, and in this scenario, identity is shaped in the face of trauma.[3] Owning as well as owned families experienced the psychological and emotional effects of slavery's ever-present violence. This framework helps us understand more about the development of identity in mixed-race slave households, and about the continuing American dilemma of race for Christians, who shape their identity as children of God, siblings to one another.

The effects of being socialized to understand Blackness as alien, separate, and inherently dangerous have always had implications for the church: how we evangelize, do missions, teach creation care and influence public policy. Many White Christians cannot identify where and how their faith tradition has prepared them to understand racism. The current era reveals much about what White Christians believe about race and whether it is an important factor. The impact of racialized ideologies ripples through all our society, yet they are not consciously understood by many, because the impact has not been sufficiently taught in the primary institutions in which we are socialized: schools and churches. Regina routinely talks to students and others who are sure that they did not have a race problem in their home communities, because those communities did not have any People of Color. Often, White people don't question why People of Color don't live in their communities. They don't know about sundown towns and restrictive covenants, not to mention the role of developers, realtors, and mortgage companies operating together to keep White neighborhoods White. Historical amnesia and ignorance, whether willful or innocent, continue to shroud our nation's racial history so that each generation of antiracist activists seemingly has to begin anew.

We need a much more nuanced understanding of the function of racial segregation—how and why it was orchestrated in the first place, and how it held together the racial hierarchy. This will in turn deepen our understanding of how it persists despite the best efforts of many people of goodwill to undo it, and of why we remain a highly segregated society.

The belief that Black and White lives are fundamentally different, as well as the inability to have empathy for Black lives, continues to have devastating results for Black people. It affects healthcare and healthcare outcomes. J. Marion Sims, lauded as the father of modern gynecology and the inventor of the vaginal speculum, honed his skills by practicing on unanesthetized enslaved Black women. Many are familiar with the Tuskegee experiment in which medical professionals and researchers, with the cooperation of the federal government, allowed syphilis, a treatable disease, to run its course among hundreds of Black men. The men were told they had something called "bad blood" and were given placebos. The forty-year so-called study resulted in the deaths of 128 men from the disease or its complications. Wives of the men were also infected, and a number of their children were born with congenital syphilis infection. More recently, a study revealed that the systematic undertreatment of Black people's pain is based on the false belief that Black people are biologically different and capable of withstanding pain to a greater degree than White people.[4]

Observations and a recent study indicate that White people routinely see and treat Black girls as older, less innocent, and less in need of support than White girls of the same age. This leads to these children being stereotyped as aggressive, disobedient, and even sexually provocative. Black girls as young as six years old have been arrested for acting out in class. The school-to-prison pipeline has affected Black children of all genders, with girls, trans, and non-binary kids being especially vulnerable.[5]

The path to violence, including structural violence, begins with dehumanization. It's easier to dehumanize someone for whom you don't have empathy, particularly if the person or group has been cast as a kind of enemy. We are familiar with the ways that propaganda has been used to gain support for war efforts; the same dynamic happens with groups that become scapegoats in their own countries. The historical record bears this out. How else to explain the photographs, for instance, of six-year-old Ruby Bridges, escorted by her mother and federal marshals as she walked into the newly desegregated William Frantz Elementary School in New Orleans with a phalanx of angry White adults jeering at her, calling her names, and threatening violence?

It's too easy to write off these crowds of angry White people in New Orleans, Little Rock, Boston, and cities and towns all over the country as fringe rebels out of step with mainstream American society. They represented what White America believed. If these adults believed that little Ruby and children like her, and their parents, were just as human and as deserving of respect and dignity, surely they would not have acted in such a manner. Yet they did. They heard sermons castigating the integrationists, and they built private Christian schools to keep the government from forcing them to have their children go to school with Black children. Of course, not all the White citizens of the towns participated in such acts. But enough did, and enough permitted it to be done in their names.

Fast-forward to the first decades of the twenty-first century, and it should seem less surprising that racial disparities still exist, that neighborhoods continue to be racially and economically segregated. The mass incarceration of People of Color, particularly Black people, costs millions if not billions of dollars. Yet incarceration rates do not correlate to crime rates but instead reflect changes in sentencing laws and policies. Black men are six times as likely to be incarcerated as White men.[6] Turning this kind of tide will take more than the good wishes of people who want to form personal relationships with People of Color as a way of defeating racism.

For one, it has proven nearly impossible to overcome the comprehensive education White people have received about Black people over the course of hundreds of years—that Black people are shiftless, lazy, and criminally inclined. Mass media is filled with these tropes, which have proved to be quite lucrative for some folks. In 2002, a game developer named David Chang put the board game Ghettopoly (yes, inspired by Monopoly—game maker Hasbro sued Chang) on the market. The game (still available to purchase online) blatantly plays on well-worn stereotypes about people who live in the ghetto, and to be specific, not just any people but Black people. Community Chest and Chance are Ghetto Stash and Hustle. The game pieces include a crack rock, a basketball, prostitutes, and pimps. This game and other novelty items might be easily dismissed by those made impatient by people who "can't take a joke," are "too sensitive," and should worry about real problems. Such responses belie ignorance about the long history of racial tropes in American popular culture. And this ignorance is not accidental and serves an important purpose—invisibilizing the effects of this long history of dehumanizing African Americans for profit and for the upholding of White supremacy. In fact, some would argue (and we do) that the primary purpose of this imagery is to keep the U.S. racial hierarchy firmly in place. They are "effective pedagogical tool[s] of dominant classes in Western culture, supporting the lessons that keep structural inequalities safely in place."[7]

In a twenty-first-century media-saturated world, we may believe such days are over. There may be a difference between what we saw then and what we see now, but racist representations of Black people still appear in music, dance, film, books, television, advertisements. The effects of generations of such imagery and the policy making that emerges from it are not easily undone. We would argue that there is a direct trajectory from these images and the narratives they support to the view of Black bodies as "out of place" and dangerous. The rash of people calling on law enforcement to control Black bodies is not new; rather, this country has practiced such behavior for hundreds of years, so it feels "normal" to police and control where these bodies can be.

The reproductions of these images in contemporary media reinscribe and reproduce the racial hierarchy so deeply embedded in U.S. history. This reality belies popular narratives that locate racist beliefs and acts solely in the past (the bad old days) and individual actions (the bad apples). The strength of these narratives is evident in the shocked reactions of people to news accounts of Black people being visibly harassed and harmed while in public spaces (or even private ones—Breonna Taylor's murder by police in her own bed).

As we learn more about the ways trauma lives in our bodies, we can begin to appreciate the depth of the toll of living within oppressive systems. Much of the work on trauma and memory began with observing and identifying post-traumatic stress disorder in war veterans. Later, there were similar observations for survivors of sexual assault and rape. Subsequent research has examined the phenomenon of historical or cultural trauma. Historical trauma is the culmination of wounding over a lifetime and across generations. The harm may be located in historical events but continues to accumulate as forms of oppression continue for subsequent generations.

Even as we learn more and more about the existence and the effects of historical trauma, a double standard exists— Which historical tragedies are worth remembering? What gets remembered as a pattern of ongoing trauma, and what gets brushed off as an unfortunate moment in history that "wasn't that bad"? Who frames the narrative? Who gets to tell our stories, and to what end?

The effects of framing the narrative in inaccurate and misleading ways extend through the generations. The example of how historians and the broader public have discussed the late 1960s and early 1970s Black Power movement makes the case. For much of the latter part of the twentieth century, historians wrote about the Black Power movement as if it had appeared out of nowhere as nothing more than an ill-conceived reaction to the traditional civil rights movement that destroyed integrationist gains by alienating White people and making radical, unrealistic demands. White historians and public commentators in particular described Black Power groups like the Black Panthers, the Nation of Islam, and the post-1966 Student Nonviolent Coordinating Committee as ill-advised, half-cocked, reactionary pseudo-revolutionaries who undermined and destroyed the hard-fought gains achieved by Martin Luther King Jr. and his associates. One of Tobin's colleagues even said to him, "They [Black Power advocates] were crazy." The idea that Black Power had ruined the possibility of what King called "the beloved community" had wide and lasting resonance.

More recent scholars, however, have shown that Black Power advocates neither brought about the demise of the civil rights movement nor stood in opposition to it. Rather, calls for

Black self-determination, respect, and economic and political autonomy emerged only *after* generations of failed attempts to address systemic racism. Between 1944 and 1963, for example, a total of 114 fair employment bills—legislative packages that would have addressed racism in employment practices in the United States—were introduced in Congress, but all of them failed. It was only after these and other integrationist efforts did not come to pass that activists began searching for another way forward. It does a disservice to the history of the Black Power movement to treat it as some kind of rebellious teenager. Instead, it offered a way forward when many roads were blocked.

Rather than disrupt progress toward dismantling racism, the Black Power movement offered multiple legacies. One of the most important has been the articulation of the difference between personal prejudice and institutional racism. In the 1967 book *Black Power* by Stokely Carmichael/Kwame Ture and Charles V. Hamilton, the authors—both Black men—made the argument that racism was fully enmeshed throughout U.S. society and democracy. Previous White scholars ranging from Alexis du Tocqueville in *Democracy in America* to Gunnar Myrdal in *An American Dilemma* had argued instead that racism in the United States was an aberration rather than an integral component. The most effective efforts at dismantling racism in predominantly White institutions have built on this fundamental observation about the ingrained nature of racism. Carmichael and Hamilton's assertion continues to resonate well into the twenty-first century.

It is not just large historical works that have maintained and encouraged White norms and standards—even children's books have upheld these structures. Regina tells this story about a book that her mother wrote:

In 1971, my mother had a children's book published, a story about my pet parakeet Snowflake. The little book chronicled the family decision to get a pet and learning how to take care of it. On the back of the book is a picture of my mother—a dark-skinned African American woman, and a blurb about how she is the mother of Regina, "the Gina in the story." However, the illustrations in the book are of a White family. In publishing then, as now (even as things have changed), Whiteness was so much the default that a Black writer's story about her Black family could not represent Blackness. The publisher either could not imagine or did not want to have a book illustrated with Black people.

Our stories are mediated through those who wield the power, those who make the decisions. While a response to this is the often-heard "Create and publish your own stories/history/narratives," this reply is not sufficient, nor is it just. We have made and do make our own. My mother went on to cofound a small publishing company that told Black stories for Black children. These efforts must continue, but we also recognize that when we create our own stories, tell our own stories, and release them out into the world, they may be embraced, but they are often not supported.

CRISES IN ANTIRACISM WORK

In our work, crises in the midst of trainings have most frequently seemed to come from those resentful about being there in the first place. For Regina, the worst rooms were the ones with academics (this was before she was an academic herself). Teaching teachers is hard work, especially when those teachers have been trained to critique and the subject matter also happens to involve their own identities. This dynamic (found not only among academics, to be sure) is why we think the level of antiracism work we do works best with people who genuinely want to be there. Of course, even then there is the possibility of conflict.

In the classroom, teaching about race can be fraught with tension, particularly during moments when "the national conversation about race" is not going well. When students resist or actively resent race as a subject matter, classroom dynamics become difficult and can feel unsafe. An example of this White resentment comes from one of Regina's experiences with an evening class of working adult students that met once a week:

I believe I was the only Person of Color in the room; I know I was the only Black person. The focus of the class was cross-cultural issues in the workplace. The lenses through which I always work are race and racism, and I use the geographical context that we all share—the United States. People who have not been educated and socialized in the United States are encouraged to make connections with their experiences in the United States and parallels/intersections of the U.S. system of race to their own countries. It gives us lots to talk about, particularly because the U.S. system of race is unique to U.S. history. It's one of the ways we know that the idea of race is a construct, because it is not exactly the same from one country to the next. This context gives us a LOT *to talk about.*

We were about three weeks into the semester, and it was time to talk very specifically about how the racialized history we inherited shows up in various disparities: education, housing, employment, incarceration rates, and on and on. It is information that causes much cognitive dissonance for those whose prior understanding of racism is that it is one's personal prejudice against people of other races.

I was using an example about the rigidity of gender norms around clothing as a way to move into a discussion about parallel ideas some folks have about the fixedness of racial categories. I noted that all the people in the room, mostly women and two men, had on pants that evening, and it was highly likely none of us thought that was unusual. However, I went on, if "Stan" here had decided to wear a dress, some people would find that curious and even upsetting because of the rules around gender and dress. Stan immediately lost it. He stood up and shouted across the room at me that he would not wear a dress; he was not a homosexual. He continued to shout that he was sick of this class, and me, blaming everything on White people and that racism was not a thing that still existed. He cited predominantly Black sports teams and President Obama and Oprah as proof that Black people were not suffering under racism. And he again made it clear that he was sick of it. After he finished, the room was silent. I could tell everyone was waiting for my response. It was a little early in the evening to call for a break, but I did. I don't know if people saw me shaking.

The information I shared in that class caused a visible crisis in that particular student. It also caused a crisis in our classroom, as I had to make a quick decision for the sake of all the other people in the room, and also to gather my wits. The third crisis was one always in the back of our minds as we do this work—What effect will this incident have on my job? Sure enough, when I got home that night I emailed the department head; the head had already been informed of the incident by the student, who had registered a complaint against me. Thankfully, I was not reprimanded. I'm not sure what that student expected—perhaps that the topic of race would be dropped from the course? The next week, we returned to the classroom and picked up where we left off. I was nervous for the rest of the course, but I did my job. At the end of the semester, a number of students expressed appreciation for what they had learned.

This was not the first time, nor would it be the last, that a White person disrupted a session because they felt personally attacked by the information. In those moments, my mind is always processing numerous things at once: how to deescalate the situation, how to be present and aware of other students in the classroom and their needs, how to stand up for myself and continue to respect the dignity of the other person. There are also my own emotions—I am simultaneously angry and, yes, afraid. Part of the fear is for the physical safety of all of us in the room; thankfully, in these situations no one has become physically violent. But I know my history. There is also the fear that maybe one day someone will complain about what I teach and how I teach it and I will lose my job. Again, I know my history, and I know that since this incident happened, more and more people are organizing to shut down critical race theory and antiracism education. Critical race theory is being misrepresented as a rewriting of history, and one of the chief complaints is that it is a way to "make White people feel bad about themselves."

THE CRISIS OF TRYING TO AVOID CONFLICT

People often worry about saying the "wrong" thing when it comes to race. It is a concern we are often asked about. People want to know how to avoid saying the wrong thing. The truth is, when matters of identity are concerned, most of us will get something wrong about identities that are not our own. We also have our own unique experiences of our identities—all Black people are not alike. So we should focus our attention on what to do after we make mistakes, and what we need to do to make it right.

Such a question can open the door to expanding under-standings of structural racism and can function as a way of creating what we sometimes call "brave space." When we are afraid to make a mistake or speak out of turn, racism becomes limited to an interpersonal realm, leaving the systemic realm untouched unless we also examine the function and power embedded in names and naming. We must deal with the struc-tural aspects of racism. Systems of oppression are kept in place when we shy away from talking about difficult things. If we don't create brave space, if we are too afraid of making a mistake, we will never get to the real work. We can remain stuck in the assumption that people are "too sensitive," or misunderstood, or that the other person isn't worth having the discussion with at all. We can easily cave in to the logic of White supremacy that says White feelings are above every-thing else and that all our energy needs to be directed at protecting White feelings. We try to anticipate and deal with this reality in the way that we structure our trainings. Our preferred way to work is in teams, or at least in pairs, and to have diversity within those teams or pairs.

Whiteness as the norm is re-created when we don't call it out. Under the guise of White supremacy, we are conditioned and socialized to understand and participate in the hierarchy: who are the experts and who we should listen to. These ideas need constant evaluation.

To show how this re-creation happens, Regina uses a classroom exercise she learned from a communication and rhetoric scholar. She instructs students to do image searches of the words *femininity* and *masculinity*. They talk in small groups about what they see and what meaning they make of it. Generally, the images that come up in relation to femininity are mostly White women; if there are women of color, they are usually light-skinned with features that are more on the side of Whiteness than on the side of other races. Masculine images serve up much of the same: mostly White men.

Next, students do an image search for *professor*. While lately this one has gotten a little better, in 2020 the search for *professor* showed mostly White men. This result is a little trickier—what the image search shows seems to correlate with the reality; most tenured and tenure-track professors are White. But professors of color do exist, as well as professors who are not men. These image searches tell a story about representation and the reality of what society thinks about othered bodies; that is, bodies that are not White and male. As we analyze what the images show us, it's clear that we know all professors are not White men, all women don't love the color pink, and so on. The exercise forces us into a conversation about images of the ideal and what that means for us as individuals and for all of us as a society. Later in the semester, when students research the demographics of their anticipated professions, we are reminded of this exercise.

Back to our training teams. In a mixed group of participants, many of the White people in the room, even if they don't admit it, even if they don't know that this is true for them, will have more trust in the White trainer over and above the Black trainer. As we've noted, our own experience bears this out. Any Black person who works in an office with mostly White people will recognize this as a phenomenon that happens with regularity at meetings: a woman or a Person of Color will put an idea on the table and get no response. Ten minutes later a White person will say the same thing and get credit for a brilliant idea.

Multiracial teams make space for this kind of racialized communication. We don't orchestrate our teams in this way to only do mind games with people; we really do want to model the possibility and the efficacy of taking advantage of diversity in all kinds of ways. We have different life experiences that can be represented. We don't agree on everything. We figure out how to work together even though this nation has conspired in all kinds of ways to make us believe that it is impossible and unnecessary for us to be able to cooperate with one another. When these conversations are held in multiracial spaces they have the potential to be contentious—as both of us have experienced in the classroom and in workshop settings. But they also have the potential to be very rich. White people in particular may never have been in such spaces—talking about race with People of Color. This is more than information sharing. It is charting new territory and building new habits.

Learning to work together in antiracist ways means understanding power imbalances. Naming Whiteness, identifying when and how it is centered and prioritized, is important. For instance, consider institutional norms around practices. We always cycle back to policies, practices, and procedures to assess current norms and to build new antiracist norms. Institutional norms should be directly related to institutional values, but unexamined norms can hinder antiracism work. Take cultural norms around meeting behavior: when are meetings scheduled, who is expected to attend, who sets the agenda—all important things to think about. But what about expected norms within the meeting? In the early years of Damascus Road, our core training team met once a year to work on the training model: to refine and update it as needed, to practice, and to bring on new trainers. We met in person for several days, coming from a number of locations around the country. One of the values of our funding organization was good stewardship of financial resources, which we all agreed to. At that time, the institutional practice around that value meant that all waking hours during a multiday meeting should be devoted to production; that is, meetings began early in the day and ended with evening sessions. This model left no room for play and, frankly, no room for the joy of being together and learning to know one another on a human level, which actually hindered us from doing our best work. We knew this was a norm that needed to change. So, put simply, we changed it.

CAN'T WE JUST BE FRIENDS?

For much of U.S. history, cross-racial friendships and relationships were scandalous—and even illegal. Subsequently, such friendships are rare. So much time and energy went into keeping these worlds separate that it should come as no surprise that the thought of integrating a school, a neighborhood, or a church would be treated with suspicion. Because of this, it is difficult to expect racism to be solved, or at least dealt with in some fashion, by forming relationships—getting to know one another. This was the model touted by many church and other religious organizations in the 1990s, marked by visiting choirs, pulpit exchanges, and common social events. Some of these efforts developed into ongoing partnerships; many, however, did not last.

We are not against the development and nurturance of personal relationships. On the contrary—we believe in the power of friendships based on mutuality and respect. Relationships built on guilt, pity, or a grudging "It's the right thing to do" will not equip us to build the kind of antiracist world we imagine. You might be thinking, "But we have to start somewhere!" And we agree. We also acknowledge the mighty task of undoing and laying aside all the baggage that hinders authentic relationships. Mutuality and respect are key;

however, stereotypes and propaganda distort the possibility of this happening.

A PRRI study in 2014, shortly after the fatal police shooting of Michael Brown, indicated that the average White American has ninety-one White friends, one Black friend, one Latino friend, one mixed-race friend, and three friends of unknown race. The average Black person has eighty-three Black friends, eight White friends, two Latino friends, and so on. For the purposes of the study, respondents were asked to name up to seven people with whom they regularly discussed important matters, and then they were asked demographic questions (what was the relationship? what were the individuals' gender, religion, and race?). Researchers concluded that 75 percent of White people surveyed had entirely White social networks, without any presence of people from minoritized identities. They argue that conversations about race in personal lives happen mostly with people who look like themselves—most White people are not socially positioned to understand the history of Black communities and police forces.

Complicity with racism, past and present, must be faced to create authentic relationships. This truth-telling is not to force people to feel bad about a past they were not there for and did not orchestrate; instead, acknowledging that "this happened, and it affects the way we live now" paves the way for building something new.

Faith communities replicate the tradition of segregation because this is the system they were born into thanks to the legacy of residential segregation, and also because of the history of Christianity's participation in the oppression of African Americans. The jewel arising from this system is the Black church, a place where Black people and Black culture flourished, despite multifaceted efforts to trivialize and demean it.

For this reason, we don't believe that a primary goal (if a goal at all) should be to integrate churches. Fortunately, antiracist practices can be in play when there is not a Person of Color in sight, and they should be.

It is telling that in Geraldo Martí's extensive study of "successful" multiracial churches (success being measured in part by maintaining a balance such that no one racial category is more than 80 percent of the total population), African Americans are the outliers, the ones who just don't really fit in. In the study, Martí acknowledges that racially conscious African Americans who bring their Black realities and concerns to multiracial congregations are dissatisfied and often do not stay. The reason: many multiracial/diversity efforts encouraged people to "transcend" race.[8] This is simply not an option for Black people in the United States. A church committed to antiracism must equip itself by recalling stories of racialization—how did people become "raced," and what does that mean in the U.S. context? For example, what does it mean for Anabaptist Christians and the way they perceive the power of the gospel in the aftermath of segregation? Such questions begin the necessary introspection for a monocultural congregation that is exploring intentional change or trying to deepen conversations within a racially diverse community.

Despite efforts to frame history differently, a tremendous amount of horror in the past has shaped the crises we encounter in the present. The temptation to gloss over the reality of a violent racist past, and religion's complicity—even dependence upon it—is attractive. Another impulse is to fast-forward to teachings on love and forgiveness, the implicit message being "forget and let's move on." Marginalized people, People of Color, and Black people are urged to forget and to sacrifice themselves for the sake of unity. But any unity that results from such a formula is false—it is the illusion of unity that comes when one party has to deny the truth of their experience and their way of knowing to get along, to move forward.

For Christians, being committed to antiracism as an act of faith offers the opportunity to authentically live *as* Christ's body—a body that is broken, battered, and bruised, and that calls into account those that participate in, or support, the battering. It is not enough to preach love as an abstract idea; Christians must embody it in bearing love and justice simultaneously within the body.

Our ideas are not brand-new. We do our work on the foundation of many who have come before us, who have worked alongside us, and whose liberation work continues today. The refusal to be silenced and dismissed because of these distorted teachings and beliefs are firmly within the tradition of marginalized people in earlier eras. This foundation includes the ability and the willingness to name oppression and it must name how religion or specific theologies have been implicated in oppression. For Christocentric Mennonites, this should begin with close scrutiny and reinterpretation of our Christology. Theologian Jacquelyn Grant argues that Jesus has been used as a tool for undergirding oppressive structures and has been imprisoned by patriarchy, White supremacy, and the privileged class.[9]

Jesus' egalitarianism and mutuality is a model for the church; it must be owned and lived out in the life of the church. This means reassessing some old practices, such as the use of images and symbols. If images of biblical figures used in liturgy and worship are only male or are only represented as White, these images must change. Whose humanity is being addressed from the pulpit? What political and cultural activities and conversations does the congregation as a whole participate in and respond to? Making spaces "multicultural" is not enough. They must also be anti-oppressive.

Critiques that challenge the tactics of the civil rights movement of the 1960s and the current Black Lives Matter movement reflect the ongoing discomfort of middle-class White Christians to face societal and religious complicity with racial oppression. The discomfort and distancing feeds the cycle of divisiveness at best, and at worst solidifies racist systems and structures. The assertion that Black and White church folk must stand together in uncomfortable spaces recalls the challenge of Fannie Lou Hamer, a veteran of the movement who assuredly tied her own activism to her Christian commitment:

> This white man who wants to stay white, and to think for the Negro . . . he is not only destroying the Negro, he is destroying himself, because a house divided against itself cannot stand and that same thing applies to America. America that is divided against itself cannot stand, and we cannot say we have all of this unity they say we have when Black people are being discriminated against in every city in America I have visited.[10]

Mrs. Hamer challenged the church to live up to its mission:

> The 1964 Summer Project was the beginning of a New Kingdom right here on earth. The kinds of people who came down from the North—from all over—who didn't know anything about us—were like the Good Samaritan. In that Bible story, the people had passed by the wounded man—like the church has passed the Negros in Mississippi—and never taken the time to see what was going on. But these people who came to Mississippi that summer—although they were strangers—walked up to our door. They started something that no one could ever stop. These people were willing to move in a non-violent way to bring a change in the South. . . .

If I had to choose today between the church and these young people—and I was brought up in the church and I'm not against the church—I'd choose these young people.[11]

Faith communities that don't explicitly align themselves with White supremacy still have work to do. We see the lack of recognition of the danger of complacency as a crisis, especially (but not only) with the rise of Christian nationalism in this country while some denominations decline in number. This is happening while the most prominent current Black liberation movement, Black Lives Matter, a movement initiated by three women of color, two of whom are queer, illustrates how intersectional analyses are informing and transforming liberation efforts. Movements for social change that promote justice are criticized for being too political, or for being political at all. Yet the foundation of politics is the organizing of our common lives. This includes the distribution of resources and protection against harm for all, especially the most vulnerable. Biblical ideas indeed.

Chapter 8

The Spiritual Work of Institutional Transformation (of Principalities and Powers)

In February 2002, a group of White activists attended a board meeting of a regional body of Mennonite Central Committee, the organization that both of us had worked for but that no longer employed us. We had helped arrange the planned intervention because the board of directors for MCC Central States had repeatedly balked at fulfilling the antiracism commitments they had made. In particular, the board had failed to hold upper-level administrators accountable for engaging in racial harassment. The risks taken by the activists and concerned constituency members who were physically present at the meeting were significant. At minimum, they risked alienation and isolation within their religious community. At worst, they risked losing their jobs because they would almost certainly carry the label of troublemaker going forward.

The result of extensive planning and background work for weeks in advance of the meeting, the intervention challenged the Central States board to not back away from dismantling racism in their community, to stop making excuses for how difficult it was to work in a predominantly White community, and to recognize the Indigenous, Black, and Latinx constituents who had historically been ignored and counted as marginal but who were growing in size and significance across the region that MCC Central States represented.

In a moment of high drama, the ten activists who had traveled to the organization's headquarters in Kansas showed up unannounced and stated that they would need fifteen minutes to speak with the board. After initially retreating from the board room to caucus, the majority-White board returned to the room and listened to the activists' demands. The activists asked that the board act on a report by an independent review team's investigation into allegations of racial harassment within MCC Central States. The investigation had found that the executive director, a program director, and the former board chair had not only actively engaged in racial harassment but then colluded to cover up their actions. But the board had done nothing to respond to the report. Instead, they had ignored the investigating team's recommendations to substantively transform the culture, decision-making patterns, accountability structures, and constituent relationships of the Central States offices. So the activists called the board to acknowledge and change the patterns of White power, privilege, and supremacy implicit throughout its staffing, program, and board structures, dismantle that institutional racism, and rebuild toward a vibrant antiracism future.

Conflict had, indeed, erupted.

Skip ahead ten years. Not only was the board itself much more diverse, but in the aftermath of the activists' intervention, the board's first move had been to hire a White man in the executive director position who had made public his commitment to stay in the position only for a limited time and who made it his first task to repair the damage done by years of neglect and abandonment of communities of color in the MCC Central States region. He likewise spoke without defensiveness or discomfort about his own White identity, privilege, and power and actively worked to build the relationships that would be necessary to maintain at least some measure of accountability.

After his planned resignation, the board then hired a new director—an African American woman—to the post. She proceeded to build a staff of White people and People of Color who were not only conversant with and committed to a principled analysis of racism and White supremacy but also aware of the history of struggle with that analysis in their geographical region. Out of conflict and crisis, a new way had opened.

In retrospect, it is doubtful that any substantive change would have come about within the Mennonite Central Committee Central States system if activists had not pressured the organization to follow through on their own internal processes. That said, change did take place. It was not necessary to tear down the organization to rebuild it entirely. And at least some of those who were present at the intervention did speak of it in both organizing and spiritual terms.

We begin this chapter on institutional transformation with this story because it raises a set of key questions about institutional transformation:

Can a predominantly White institution transform itself without externally prompted crisis?

Is it possible to initiate internal change without starting over from scratch?

What role does spirituality play in the work of dismantling institutional racism?

In this chapter we explore all of these questions and offer the insight we have gained from our work walking alongside predominantly White institutions as they have sought to claim and implement effective antiracist commitments. In so doing, we discuss the idea of principalities and powers as a theological and organizing phenomenon. We identify seven principles and three first steps that we have seen be most effective in predominantly White organizations. We offer a chart for identifying the way forward. And we give some examples of organizations that have, in fact, found ways to change.

OF PRINCIPALITIES AND POWERS

American theologian Walter Wink wrote extensively and with great sophistication about the inner and outer representations of social systems. In addition to the structural dimension evident in boards and edifices and personnel policies, Wink asserted that those same systems had spiritual dimensions—a gestalt, if you will—that needed to be addressed as surely as did the more physically and organizationally apparent dimensions. To fail to do so, said Wink, was to ignore how and why those institutions proved so difficult to change.

In his classic text *Naming the Powers*, Wink delineates the language offered in the Christian New Testament to describe these inner dimensions. From the largest perspective, the principalities and powers are the essence, the psychological and spiritual fabric, of a large system like law enforcement or a specific institution within it, such as a local jail. Demons, Wink adds, are a way of anthropomorphizing the power emanated at both the psychic and spiritual levels by organizations within those systems or specific individuals who inhabit them as they are engaged in the work of dominating others.

In the same vein, Wink names gods as the social archetypes—those recurring cultural symbols, trends, and icons that define and represent how we define good and evil—that shape our interpretation of the world around us and, through that process of socialization, set up powerful reality-defining screens in our consciousness. He then states that the idea of evil incarnate—represented as Satan or the devil in multiple spiritual traditions—is the coalescing of power knit together whenever individuals within those institutions and systems choose to place the pursuit of injustice, greed, and self-aggrandizement ahead of the values of human connection, selflessness, and equity. The expression of that power ebbs and wanes according to the level of that expressed refusal to opt for justice.

In short, Wink offers a way to think about and respond to a religious idiom and set of symbols that left many in the modern era suspicious and skeptical. Rather than hocus-pocus popular culture cartoons of impish devils and wispy angels, under Wink's tutelage the principalities and powers took on a complexity, nuance, and expression that not only made sense but also pointed to the importance of staying engaged with the spiritual dimension. He provided a language for recognizing just how essential it was to take the spiritual dimension seriously.

But his work did one thing more. Wink also provided a language for recognizing that it was possible to redeem those institutions and systems. Just because the principalities and powers existed and added a challenging dimension to the work of dismantling racism did not mean they were permanent. They could be fundamentally altered and transformed. Simply naming them, describing how they operated, and removing the power of their unconscious hegemony was a critical step forward in that process of transformation. Once stripped of the ability to operate unseen, those spiritual dimensions of systems and institutions lost some of their agency. It is much more difficult to shape the unconscious when the process of that shaping is laid bare than when it operates without comment or description.

What we find particularly helpful from Wink's work as it has informed our efforts to dismantle racism is the recognition not only that it is possible to transform the institutions with whom we work but also that transformation requires more than just structural realignment. Wink has reminded us—along with the stated grassroots observations of long-time change agents in the Black freedom struggle like Septima Poinsette Clark, Ella Baker, Bayard Rustin, Fannie Lou Hamer, and many others—that we need to be prepared for the kind of spiritual struggle that can shake the heart and the gut as well as demand the best of our intellectual focus. It was not by accident, for example, that Mrs. Hamer spoke to national political committees *and* led Student Nonviolent Coordinating Committee members in singing spiritual songs. She knew what would be demanded of those who resisted and sought to bring about change. She sought to prepare them accordingly.

RESPONDING TO THE POWERS

But what do those change efforts actually then look like? How do we engage in transforming predominantly White institutions so that they can live out an antiracist vision? What needs to happen for that to take place?

Since we are so often asked this very question, we've stripped down the many possible pathways to a set of seven principles and initial three steps that we have seen bear significant fruit over the years. Their actual implementation will look quite different based on their particular settings, internal dynamics, and institutional histories, but the principles that guide those actions are identifiable, consistent, and straightforward.

And so we start, once again, with a story.

In the spring of 1960, a dozen or so Black high school students in Danville, Virginia, demanded that they be allowed to use the public library. The library, a segregated facility revered by the local White community, had hosted the final meeting of the Confederate government before the Civil War ended. In the face of intense White hostility, the students held a sit-in at the library. In response the city government closed the public library and a new "Danville Library Foundation" planned to open a Whites-only private one that in turn invited more protest. By the fall, the public library had reopened but—in a particular show of disdain and ongoing racism—had removed all patron chairs from the facility.

Change—of a sort—had come to the Danville Public Library. At some point they put the chairs back. We have yet to determine when. Today the Danville Public Library is open to all.

But as in the case of the story that opens this chapter about Mennonite Central Committee Central States, the question remains about how that process took place and what might have made it less likely that crisis would, once again, be required to bring about change. At the least, the anecdote illustrates the need to figure out ways to make that kind of crisis less of a prerequisite for substantive and sustainable change.

Racism operates in so many different ways that it can be confusing to understand how they fit together or how to respond to them. Why we would even invest time trying to transform seemingly well-meaning and apparently benign institutions like MCC Central States or the Danville Public Library is not immediately apparent. It often seems much more important to push back against the use of racial epithets or Grand Wizards who wear white sheets. To help orient our actions, it will be helpful to at least briefly discuss the many manifestations that racism takes in society. Tobin's wife is a nurse. She has helped us understand just how important it is to get the diagnosis right before we prescribe a therapy. We have to know what kind of racism we are confronting before we develop a strategy to deal with it.

Racism looks quite different if it is being expressed in a more public or private vein or in a more individual or collective one. And it takes many, many forms. The strategy to confront an individual microaggression in private is very different from responding to ongoing collective acts of housing segregation in public. Distinct expressions of racism call for distinct responses to racism. We have developed the charts on page 159 to help us visualize what these distinct expressions of racism look like and to note the full range of options for responding to those forms based on our assessment of where and how those expressions of racism manifest.

In our work together, we have focused specifically and intentionally on institutional transformation, dismantling those parts of institutional life that are not as visible—hence more private—but are yet fully collective. We have done so because once predominantly White institutions are equipped to dismantle racism in their own houses, they can be effective partners in the broader work of dismantling racism in society.

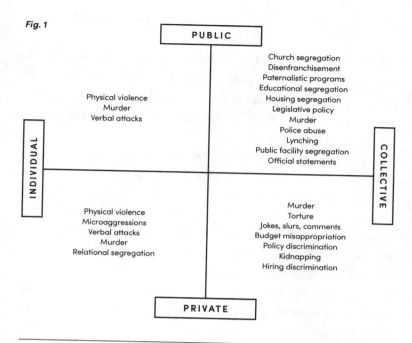

Fig. 1

PUBLIC

Church segregation
Disenfranchisement
Paternalistic programs
Educational segregation
Housing segregation
Legislative policy
Murder
Police abuse
Lynching
Public facility segregation
Official statements

Physical violence
Murder
Verbal attacks

INDIVIDUAL

COLLECTIVE

Physical violence
Microaggressions
Verbal attacks
Murder
Relational segregation

Murder
Torture
Jokes, slurs, comments
Budget misappropriation
Policy discrimination
Kidnapping
Hiring discrimination

PRIVATE

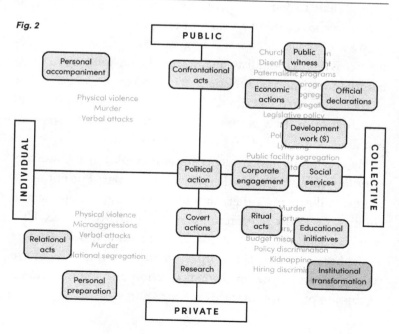

Fig. 2

PUBLIC

Personal accompaniment

Confrontational acts

Public witness

Economic actions

Official declarations

Development work ($)

Physical violence
Murder
Verbal attacks

INDIVIDUAL

Political action

Corporate engagement

Social services

COLLECTIVE

Physical violence
Microaggressions
Verbal attacks
Murder
Relational segregation

Covert actions

Ritual acts

Educational initiatives

Relational acts

Research

Institutional transformation

Personal preparation

PRIVATE

That is where we want to continue to invest our energies. It is where we see the greatest potential for both individual and collective transformation in the inner and outer manifestations of systemic racism with all the representations of the principalities and powers intact.

Even as we have focused on dismantling racism within institutions, we are aware that White nationalism is once again resurging. One of the most devastating effects of that resurgence is that so much energy has gone into defeating its many expressions. That work is essential. Yet the energy that goes into defeating White nationalists and other racist hate groups is energy not spent on dismantling the systemic racism that creates such deep-seated racial inequities in access to housing, education, transportation, jobs, and healthcare. Far more lives are lost each day to the manifestations of systemic racism than to hate-based, White nationalist expressions of racism in the course of a year—or ten years.

We are convinced that it is time we stopped just being reactive to White nationalists and started being proactive in dismantling institutional racism. It is exactly in the midst of that challenging, often less dramatic work of internal institutional transformation that we need the greatest access to spiritual resources to see our efforts sustained over time.

By this point it is evident that we employ the word *dismantling* racism. That is deliberate on our part but not at all unique. Like many other antiracism training groups in the country, we know that racism was "mantled" over time. That is, it was deliberately put in place. Dismantling it will take just as deliberate action. The word *dismantling* reminds us of the twin concepts of the intentional creation and the intentional disruption of racism that this work requires.

There are many paths we can take to dismantle racism. The principles that we articulate here are not the only ones. We offer them at this point because they provide a concrete, direct, and—at least in our experience—effective way to build on intentions and realize the change that we seek. The principles are also the best way we know to act with integrity and be consistent with the spiritual grounding that can sustain and foster us amid effective institutional change.

PRINCIPLE 1: ANTICIPATE AND WORK THROUGH THREE PARADIGM SHIFTS

First, we have observed that predominantly White institutions need to prepare and support their staff and constituency to move through three paradigm shifts. The greater clarity that members can articulate in their analysis of racism, the more effective they can be in addressing the forms that it takes. The three paradigm shifts are (1) to move from an assumption that racism is no longer present in contemporary society—it is not a thing of the past—to acknowledging that racism is present with us and has been for a long time; (2) to shift from the assumption that racism exists only to harm People of Color to the understanding that the purpose of racism is to maintain White power and privilege; and (3) to change from assuming that racism affects only People of Color to recognizing that the receipt of White power and privilege shapes White people.

In our early work at dismantling racism, we paid a great deal of attention to that first paradigm shift. In short, we tried very hard to convince White people that racism was not just a thing of the past. We no longer expend as much energy doing so. People of Color have been testifying to the ongoing reality of racism for many, many years. The advent of social media and the widespread availability of cell phones with cameras has amplified that testimony, but some members of our society—through what we can only describe as a willful act of ignorance—continue to discredit that evidence. The data is overwhelming. Acknowledging the present reality of racism is the first step toward effectively dismantling it. You can't change a problem that you don't admit exists.

We have observed consistently over time that members of the White community most often describe racism in terms of the harm it does to People of Color. The second paradigm shift—recognizing that racism has been designed to maintain power and privilege for White people—is often more challenging than the first paradigm shift, but it is no less necessary, because as we noted earlier, our diagnosis determines our therapy. If we assume that racism is only hurting People of Color, then we will design responses that only attempt to repair those communities and leave the ongoing realities of racism, White supremacy, and White power untouched and unexamined. In the process, the efforts to dismantle that racism are themselves compromised and undermined and often move forward with a paternalism born of the very White supremacy that remains intact even while trying to undermine and push back against racism.

The third paradigm shift is even more demanding. The idea that the receipt of White power and privilege shapes White people in ways that can distort one's self-image and make it very difficult to enter into sustained, collaborative relationships across racial lines leaves many people even more threatened. We have again observed that members of the White community are uncomfortable with and resist naming their identity as White people at all—let alone exploring how that White identity is shaped by racism that grants White people power and privilege and, in the process, leaves them expecting the receipt of that unearned privilege from the systems of racism to the extent that their spiritual muscles atrophy, they become dependent on racism, and their walk and witness in the world is fundamentally compromised. The movement back toward integrity and wholeness is a movement that begins with recognizing that the receipt of White power and privilege damages White people even while claiming to offer superiority and sustenance.

And so the question is this: How can predominantly White institutions and their staff, leadership, and boards not only work through these paradigm shifts themselves but also become part of transforming society to make these transitions as well?

PRINCIPLE 2: ANALYZE WHITE STRUCTURES

The next principle follows from these paradigm shifts. All work to dismantle institutional racism needs to start from the analysis that predominantly White institutions have been structured to serve White people. In the antiracism trainings we offer, we spell out the history of how the major systems of the United States were structured to serve White people. In one training piece, we trace the White supremacist processes at play in the development of those systems during a period in which only White men were considered human by the laws and founding documents of this country, a period that accounts for more than 70 percent of the history of European Americans' presence in the United States. Those systems continued to foster institutions mandated to serve White people under a legal structure that declared there would be separate and equal services for those not deemed White but that never appropriated the funds or the resources to make them either truly separate or truly equal. Even after those laws of segregation were overturned, the institutions that had been set up to serve White people did not change the manner and method of their being. Once we have oriented ourselves to recognizing what the focus of our work needs to be—creating institutions that serve all people so that they no longer serve just White people—then we have the opportunity to be truly effective.

PRINCIPLE 3: START WITH WHAT IS USUALLY IGNORED

Third, the work of dismantling racism does not begin where most people think it does. A cryptic statement, we know. What we mean is that most predominantly White institutions begin addressing racism by simply trying to become more colorful. They acknowledge that their staffing and board membership are too White—if not exclusively White—and seek to change that by diversifying those memberships. However, such efforts need to be coupled with deliberate and sustained efforts to go deeper into the organization; to institute antiracist values into the mission, identity, and purpose; to address how the structures of the organization are set up; to reconsider and reshape assumptions about the organization's constituency. In short, the less public, more subtle, and most powerful elements of predominantly White organizations are those which are most often ignored, invisible, and avoided. We aim to support those same institutions to go deeper and thereby work in ways that have proven more effective.

PRINCIPLE 4: EVALUATE RESULTS BEFORE INTENTIONS

Our fourth principle turns toward implementation of these ideas. In the midst of doing this work, we need to evaluate by results, not intentions. For too long, White institutions have simply said, "But we tried. We meant to do better." Effective antiracism work evaluates what actually happens because of our efforts, not just what we meant to have happened. This is a profoundly spiritual principle as well. It speaks of the need to strip away pretense. To no longer hide behind bureaucracy and the inauthentic language of the press release. Shifting to open, honest, and direct statements about the actual outcomes of our efforts to dismantle racism offers a way to come clean, receive direct feedback, and make our way forward unencumbered by false claims of good intentions presented as concrete results. Such honesty—in the collective sense as well as the individual—stems from a courage and a piercing commitment to truth born of grounded spiritual practice. It seldom appears without some connection to those practices.

PRINCIPLE 5: ESTABLISH ACCOUNTABILITY TO COMMUNITIES OF COLOR

We have invested much in figuring out how to embody this fifth principle in the work that we have done as an interracial training and writing team. This is the statement that we make and, as we indicated earlier, try to embody in our work: White people need to work with White people while in accountable relationships to People of Color. Especially in the moment where we are now, we cannot be asking People of Color to do all the work for those who are White. What this means is that White people in predominantly White institutions and elsewhere need to take risks, speak up, call for antiracism training, and be part of the solution while being willing to listen to and honor the leadership of People of Color in doing so.

In our relationship, we have long recognized the importance of talking through, considering, and evaluating carefully how we will present, in what order, and with which content. Those discussions have been unfailingly honest, direct, and nested within a now decades-long history of struggling together, making mistakes, and learning from them. At the same time, we remain committed to also affirming that in this context Regina retains veto power over those decisions. This practice has been important to put in place a structural brake—even within a trust-filled relationship—on the power and privilege that flows Tobin's way when we are working in public and, at times, even in our private interactions. Rather than create or foster distrust, it has worked to stabilize, sustain, and make it possible to work together across racial lines even as we continue to recognize that Tobin's primary work will be to walk alongside and offer support to other White people as they seek to dismantle racism and Regina's primary work will be to do the same with members of the Black, Indigenous, and People of Color communities.

PRINCIPLE 6: REMEMBER THE MONEY MATTERS

The sixth principle that we identify is that the money matters. As a basic sociological principle, we know that the actual values of an institution are expressed not so much in what they say as in how they spend their money. It is one thing for a predominantly White organization—whether a church, nonprofit, or corporation—to make a statement in support of the celebration of the proclamation of the emancipation from slavery known as Juneteenth (which is a good thing). It is another for a predominantly White organization to invest the necessary financial and personnel resources to equip themselves to enact the values celebrated on Juneteenth. To understand the actual values of an institution, all you have to do is follow the money. Again, this principle has profoundly spiritual roots. Religious communities have for centuries called their adherents to match their stated values with their stated actions. Even when it proves costly. Especially when it proves costly. Those religious groups have supported integrity. Investing funds in ways that match our values moves us in that direction. Our spiritual values sustain us as we do so.

PRINCIPLE 7: PRACTICE MUTUAL SUPPORT

The seventh and final principle that we promote is to state simply that supporting each other is essential. We have noted in particular that as White people begin to work at dismantling racism, they often attempt to prove their antiracism credentials by demonstrating how harsh and unforgiving they can be toward other White people. It becomes a form of distancing one's self from members of one's racial group, a way to say, "Look. That is not me. I am not one of the bad White people. I'm a good White person. Just watch how mean I can be to them." Rather, we promote the guidance of antiracism educator and organizer Dody Matthias, who promotes the principle "Leave no one behind." The work of White people is not to demonstrate distance or separation from other White folk. Rather, it is to demonstrate empathy for and walk alongside White people so that our collective antiracism efforts can be improved all around. The spiritual practice in all of this is to find ways to maintain human connection and relationship while also calling White people forward to become their better selves. A balancing act if ever there was one.

These principles take time and practice to implement. But we know from experience that they make a difference. A faculty union executive board used these principles to develop their own guidelines for taking antiracist action, hired two antiracist consultants to give them feedback, and then changed the nature of their board work. The communications department of a major denomination's mission agency used them to completely transform how they wrote about their work with international partners. Where once they focused on the agency and actions taken by their predominantly White service worker corps in the framing and cropping of the photos they featured in their work—for example—they shifted to orienting the perspective to the abilities, initiatives, and full partnership of the communities in which their volunteers were hosted. A reuse-it shop invested time and attention in reframing their assumptions about and attitudes toward their customer and client base and began to develop partnerships with local Indigenous communities by attending their events rather than always asking the tribes to come to theirs.

The question is not whether these principles are effective but whether a given institution will hold their employees accountable for implementing and maintaining these kinds of principles. When consulting with organizations interested in enacting antiracist values, we note that the three most common indicators of success are a *long-term antiracist vision*— that is being able to explain to others in simple, direct, and straightforward language the kind of organization that you want to become; *accountability* in some kind of direct and concrete form to Black, Indigenous, and People of Color communities for the work that the organization does; and regular, periodic *evaluation of staff* at all levels of the organization that includes assessment of their ability to integrate antiracist values in their work performance. Where groups have implemented those practices, they have found success.

FIRST THREE STEPS

But participants in our seminars and workshops also ask us for direction as to what initial, practical steps a predominantly White group can take to start their antiracist journey. So we have boiled down our recommendations to three actions that we have seen prove effective time and again.

First, we encourage predominantly White organizations to make public their commitment to antiracism through their mission statement, signage, and online presence. People of Color tell us again and again that it makes a difference what a predominantly White institution says about itself and how it says it. Of course, those words can be cosmetic and performative, offering nothing more than a cynical proclamation of the message of the moment. But they also hold the potential to help hold the organization accountable to do what they say they will do. Whether words on paper or words onscreen, those words can also shape expectations in powerful ways.

At one point in the summer of 2020, the leaders of a historic preservation committee in a midsize city from the Northwest approached us about how best to make a statement about "racial mistakes of the past." We told them that they needed to be about the business of crafting a new antiracist narrative, one that would require boldly and unflinchingly confronting the racism of the past. And so we pushed them to clearly label those "racial mistakes of the past" as racism while also publicly claiming their commitment to an antiracist future. Internal statements about racism do very little good if they remain internal. It is only by making our antiracist commitments public that we can be held accountable for living up to those statements.

The second central action that we encourage predominantly White groups to take focuses on how we think about and conceive of racism. We recommend that institutions develop a common language and framework for talking about and working to dismantle racism. We need a way to bridge the gap that emerges almost every time White people and People of Color try to talk about racism. White people focus on the interpersonal. People of Color pay attention to the systemic. Offering antiracism training to staff and board members makes it possible to develop a common vocabulary, common analysis, and common practice and vision. There are many ways to make this happen. We do caution groups when assessing which training partners to hire to be sure that they actually talk about racism and bring a systemic analysis to the table. The business world in particular is filled with diversity experts who talk around but do not actually address the problem of racism. In many ways, saying that you will do something about racism but then only tiptoeing past the problem is worse than doing nothing at all. It is a particularly egregious form of gaslighting to say that you have addressed racism while lifting up the example of a training experience that was not direct, effective, or focused on the problem of racism itself.

A third concrete step we promote is to do an antiracism audit that involves patrons, professionals, and People of Color. This is a tool to focus an organization's attention, reflection, and action on the full breadth of their institutional structures through both internal and external conversation led and facilitated by skilled antiracism staff in diverse but focused and efficient teams. The antiracism process can take as little as two months and provides a starting point for the honest reckoning and thorough evaluation needed to develop a long-term antiracism plan. Institutions have used such antiracism audits to change the nature of their relationships with the local community, to initiate new programming, to craft physical and virtual spaces, and to rethink the ways and means of the organization's culture, removing elements of White supremacy culture in the process.

MARKERS OF ANTIRACIST INSTITUTIONAL TRANSFORMATION

In antiracism audits that we have been a part of, we use the following chart to help groups think about the sequence of their actions based on a self-identification of where they are in the work of their organization. It looks like this.

	1 OVERT	2 NEUTRAL	3 COSMETIC
Identity & Mission	Claims exclusion	Claims colorblindness	States multicultural commitments
Organizational Culture	Celebrates White supremacy culture (WSC)	Unaware of WSC	Denies WSC
Program Initiatives	Intends to serve only White people	Claims program neutrality	Initiatives focus on celebration of diversity
Staffing Patterns	Whites only	Token representation	Staff less than 20% People of Color; short-term stays
Accountability	To Whites exclusively	Deemed unnecessary	"Safe" BIPOC connections
Structure & Constituency	Designed for White control and access	Keeps control and access hidden	Leaves control and access untouched

	4 PROCLAMATION	5 IMPLEMENTATION	6 REALIZATION
Identity & Mission	Claims antiracist commitments; articulates core principles	Promotes antiracist commitments and enacts core principles	Fulfills antiracist commitments and principles
Organizational Culture	Acknowledges WSC	Addresses WSC	No longer practices WSC
Program Initiatives	Programs address hierarchy, privilege, and oppression	Programs address systemic inequality	Programs fully embody antiracist values
Staffing Patterns	Goals for staff greater than 20% People of Color; mid-term stays	Staff above 20% People of Color; stable duration	Sustained staffing; balanced representation
Accountability	Commits to accountability	Implements accountability	Fully integrates accountability
Structure & Constituency	Examines and analyzes control and access	Engages in restructuring to undermine White power structures	Realizes restructuring

The chart does two primary things. First, it points institutions to the six areas in need of attention in an antiracism audit: identity and mission, organizational culture, program initiatives, staffing patterns, accountability, and structure and constituency. Just as importantly, it suggests a sequence in which they are most effectively addressed. The work starts by first attending to issues around the organization's identity and mission in order to lay a foundation for all that follows. By claiming an antiracist identity, groups are then able to focus on transforming their culture out of patterns of White supremacy. Shifting away from White supremacy culture makes changes in programming possible that in turn lay the groundwork for the possibility of sustainable hiring of members of the Black, Indigenous, and People of Color communities. Those staffing patterns then allow for establishing meaningful accountability relationships within and without the organization to People of Color. The work that follows allows for attention to structure and constituency of the organization.

In addition to suggesting a sequence for this kind of transformative work, the chart also notes that all predominantly White organizations start somewhere on a continuum of growth and have somewhere to go. The movement from an organization that is neutral or cosmetic in its pursuit of diversity goals to one that first proclaims, then implements, and finally realizes their antiracism goals follows key stages, each with their own particular challenges. For example, the movement from the cosmetic to the proclamation stage is often the most volatile when addressing any of the identified areas. This is because of the shift from simply talking about diversity in a general sense to actually implementing it with specific and direct attention to the issues of power, privilege, and oppression. If an organization can get through those stages and maintain forward momentum, they have a significant chance of seeing the antiracism work through. If they don't make that shift from cosmetic to proclamation, the work falls back into the initially more comfortable but ultimately more destructive stage of surface-level commitment, one that People of Color immediately recognize as inauthentic, alienating, and manipulative.

We have watched organizations move forward. We have watched them fall back. The key value that made a difference for their path was whether they had successfully integrated an analysis of systemic racism throughout their organization. An antiracist audit is often an effective tool to do a reality check as to whether that analysis has been made widespread enough to offer the best possible chance of supporting further work and movement.

It is impossible to say what would have happened at the public library in Danville, Virginia, if they had been equipped to start dismantling racism before they were pressured into desegregating their facility. We do know that taking more proactive steps would have demanded much less of the African American community there. We also know that any work that decouples crisis from the work of dismantling racism holds great promise for success. When groups recognize that antiracism efforts will make their congregation, synagogue, nonprofit, business, educational organization, government agency—or whichever kind of predominantly White organization not represented in this list—stronger, the chance for success increases all the more. As we often tell the groups with whom we work, "Racism gets in the way of us doing our jobs. We want to help you get racism out of the way so that you can do your job better."

Finding ways to marshal the human and financial resources to engage in the work of dismantling racism without street

marches or demonstrations can be challenging because historically it has usually been only in those moments that Whiteness
and the racism that undergirds it has been made visible to the
White population as a whole, or at least those who are paying
attention. But that is exactly why pursuing an antiracist spirituality is such an essential component of the work of dismantling racism. The practices and principles we have described
here have the best chance of coming to fruition when they are
grounded in spiritually significant awareness of the principalities and powers that sustain White supremacy. All we have
tried to do in this chapter is provide some language, following
Walter Wink's articulation, to engage those powers and make
a difference in doing so.

Rather than set spiritual questions and the disciplines and
practices of spirituality on a shelf separated from and above
the day-to-day challenges of being human and operating within
institutions, we emphasize again and again that the spiritual
dimension as we have described it here counts. It matters. It
needs our attention.

The integrity of the work we do in the institutions to which
we belong depends on us finding ways to make those connections and follow them through over time.

Chapter 9

The Spirituality of Individuality versus a Collective Approach

When classes or workshops on dismantling racism conclude, White participants offer one comment more than any other. It is simply this: "I am overwhelmed."

This happens every time.

Among ourselves, we have talked about this pattern and pondered what it means. It is not so much the consistency of the response as it is its context. For generations, members of the African American, Latinx, Asian American, and Indigenous communities have lived and died with the realities of racism that the overwhelmed White participants have only just encountered in a five-week introductory course or a weekend-long intensive workshop. On the one hand, we understand how any given intense encounter with a new body of knowledge can leave one feeling at sea. On the other, the contrast between the individual statement about feeling over-whelmed and the centuries-old collective reality of communi-ties of color having to deal with racism on a regular basis is rather stark.

We are not sure whether to be encouraged that White participants are at least feeling something about racism or despondent that there so often seems to be a lack of aware-ness about how a statement by a White person regarding feel-ing overwhelmed by racism would come across to a Person of Color.

In either case, that consistent pattern emerges from the default assumption that seems to permeate White people in particular but increasingly can be found among communities of color as well. The assumption seems to be that the work of dismantling racism must be an individual one. That it must be gigantic in its proportions. And that only those with Herculean strength are worthy and capable of the task. The thought of a collective response, like a collective spirituality, is foreign.

In this chapter, we want to make the idea of a collective response more familiar, exploring what it can look like. We will tie that kind of response to a collective spirituality. And we offer some thoughts on what we have seen effective in those places where collective responses have emerged.

To be sure, we do not want to deny the key role that indi-viduals have played in bringing about change. Whether refer-encing the organizing skills of Ella Baker, the legal genius of Pauli Murray, or the strategical interventions of Bayard Rus-tin, the history of the Black freedom struggle—for instance—would be very different were it not for the courageous and unwavering commitment of individuals like these. But even in these instances, standout individuals have emerged from communities that supported them, shaped them, and fostered the brilliance of their contributions.

If we are to be prepared for the long-term work of dismantling racism, we need to understand and be situated in communities of struggle and celebration that nurture, support, challenge, and resist and resist again.

THE COMMUNITY AT BURGLUND HIGH SCHOOL

Rhetoric about community has been around a long time. But it is one thing to lift up the theory of community and collective response. It is another thing to make that practical and apply it. To begin our exploration of antiracist spirituality that is grounded in community and made collective as much as it is expressed individually, we will start with a specific example of that antiracist collectivity made manifest.

This story begins when students at Burglund High School in McComb, Mississippi, in 1961 heard of their principal's decision to expel their classmate Brenda Travis for having participated in a protest against segregation at that town's Greyhound bus station. When they heard the news, more than 110 students from this all-Black, segregated school got up from the assembly in which their principal announced Travis's expulsion and marched to city hall. By the time they arrived, word of their march had spread so quickly that not only were FBI agents and newspaper reporters present to observe, but a White mob more than equal to their number stood around them holding chains and pipes. Undeterred, the students stood before the crowd and faced city hall. Then Hollis Watkins—an eighteen-year-old student—walked to the steps of city hall, knelt on the ground, raised his left hand to the sky as was common in many Black Baptist churches, and began to recite the Lord's Prayer. Along with some members of the mob, the police stepped in and dragged Watkins to jail.

The action could have stopped right there. Not only was the crowd threatening the young marchers, but the weapon-bearing town residents were reserving a special ire for a White southern Student Nonviolent Coordinating Committee member by the name of Bob Zellner. The White mob would soon savagely beat Zellner. The youth, too, risked physical beating and arrest with the prospect of an unknown amount of jail time.

But the next student in line behind Watkins did not stop. He was part of the community. He did as Watkins had done before him. He stepped forward to the city hall steps, knelt there, and began to pray. Again the police stepped in and took him away. He was then followed by a fresh set of high school students. The praying and the escorting and the peri- odic beating by the mob continued until every one of those marchers went to jail. Those under eighteen spent three days incarcerated. Those eighteen and over spent thirty-nine days inside a cell. After refusing to sign a pledge that they would not participate in any future civil rights demonstrations, most of the students were denied readmission to their school. Once again, they did not stop to ask how they could possibly con- tinue in the struggle as individuals in the face of this kind of retribution. Once released from jail, they still could not return to their school. Their principal had expelled them. And so, as a group, they enrolled in and attended J. P. Campbell Junior College in Jackson, nearly eighty miles away.

That this was a moment of high drama cannot be denied. That it comes to us from the pages of history books is also undeniable. But to our minds that makes the story no less essential as an example of the power of collective action and collective spiritual practice. Consider the elements at play here. This was no intervention of a lone prophet. The students responded to the leadership initially offered by Brenda Travis, but even she did not act alone in her initial participation at the Greyhound station protest. When they did act, the students were supported by older SNCC organizers, who were in turn sustained by longtime Black organizers and resisters such as Amzie Moore and others. The high drama of the encounter at city hall was made possible only because of this kind of generational, collective, sustained community.

The high drama of the moment was in turn sacralized by the students' choice to kneel and pray. During a summer seminar on the civil rights movement, Tobin had the opportunity to ask Hollis Watkins why he and his fellow high school protestors had chosen to pray when they arrived at city hall. Mr. Watkins's response was telling. He simply said, "Why, because it was the thing to do, of course." This is the statement of someone immersed in a community where prayer was common, expected, and collective. Regardless of any individual statement of belief or conviction, or of any particular evidence of a given student's spiritual practices at home, the fact is that they shared a common vocabulary about prayer and the powerful and appropriate role it could play in raising one's voice in public, in speaking back against the inhuman power of segregation and the White supremacy that sustained it. The students were able to offer a collective witness because, at least in part, they shared a measure of collective spiritual grounding.

EASTER 1963—THE DAY BULL CONNOR DIDN'T GET HIS WAY

Another moment of high drama from the civil rights movement again emphasizes the importance and possibility of collective resistance. This civil rights story did not end with arrests or

violence, however. But it did involve prayer. And it did take
place on Easter—April 14, 1963, to be exact—in the midst of
the violence and crisis of the efforts by the Southern Christian
Leadership Conference (SCLC) to desegregate Birmingham,
Alabama, that city where White public safety commissioner
"Bull" Connor regularly turned attack dogs and firehoses on
nonviolent demonstrators.

This moment of collective witness began with a march
some five thousand strong—all local Birmingham members
of the African American community there, all dressed in their
Sunday best after worshiping on that Easter morning. The
marchers had gathered at New Pilgrim Baptist Church and
were headed to the downtown Birmingham jail where Martin
Luther King Jr. sat in a jail cell. They planned to pray and
sing songs outside the jailhouse and return to New Pilgrim,
but two blocks from the jail, Bull Connor had set up a roadblock. Firefighters stood behind the double-powered firehoses
that Connor had special-ordered to better pummel and push
back demonstrators. As the marchers approached, police dogs
growled and pulled against their leashes.

Connor yelled, "Disperse this crowd. Turn this
group around."

In response the march leaders asked those assembled behind
them to kneel to the pavement and pray. As a group, they did
so. The sound of audible prayers began to rise as women in
the group started praying. One participant described those
prayers as "an old-fashioned kind of long-meter moan, mixed
with singing." The volume of their prayers—ones practiced
and tuned from hours spent praying together—began to rise.
Connor remained unmoved.

Then Rev. Charles Billups, a longtime leader of the local
Black freedom struggle, jumped to his feet and yelled, "The

Lord is with this movement! Off your knees. We're going to the jail!" In response, those in the front row rose from their feet and walked toward the barricades as Bull Connor hollered, "Stop 'em, stop 'em!" Undaunted, they approached the barricades together—en masse. As a group.

In response, not one person on the other side of the roadblock moved. Not the police. Not the firefighters. Even the attack dogs grew calm. Connor redoubled his efforts. He yelled, "Turn on the hoses, turn on the hoses!" But no one responded to his order. One firefighter dropped the hose he only moments before had been ready to turn on the demonstrators.

The crowd marched through the barricades, brushing past the silent officers, singing, "I want Jesus to walk with me." They walked slow and serious until assembled at the jail. They sang for those in the jail. Then, they went back home without incident.[1]

This story is in some ways a dangerous one to tell. Seldom were the outcomes of civil rights protests so, well, miraculous. The events in Birmingham on Easter of 1963 were in no way typical of collective actions taken there or in just about any other event in the long Black freedom struggle. By contrast, on June 10 of that same year in Danville, Virginia, a group of Black residents marched to city hall and gathered there to pray in an act of protest against Danville's ongoing practices of segregation. On that day in that city as the demonstrators knelt on the pavement, the police attacked them with clubs and turned firehoses on them until they lay bloodied, bruised, and beaten on the ground. Many had broken limbs; nearly all had open wounds. One observer described the injuries he saw in graphic detail: eyes swollen, heads split open, swellings rising two inches above the scalp. When a Student Nonviolent Coordinating Committee member called

SNCC's Atlanta office to report on the events, she broke down and wept. Later she explained, "You were supposed to be so brave. You weren't supposed to cry."[2]

This too was the result of spiritually grounded, collective action.

The outcomes are not guaranteed.

But even so, it is the process that counts.

These stories are marked by a community of people coming together and making the decision that they will act, they will do so together, and their spirituality will shape and inform not just what they will do, but how they will do it. Dropping to the pavement to pray in the midst of facing down segregationists was part tactic—SCLC staffer Andrew Young remembered thinking that asking the marchers to pray would at the very least buy them some time—but was also the natural outgrowth of a collective history of turning to prayer for solace, strength, and sustenance on a daily basis. Those who prayed in Danville and McComb as well as hundreds of others throughout the early 1960s phase of the civil rights movement were praying because it was one of the most concrete and consistent practices, as well as one of the most portable ones, that they could bring to bear from the central institution of the Black community. They were, in essence, bringing the foundational collective spiritual practice of their community to bear on the core collective social struggle of their day.

And that is the lesson that these stories perhaps best offer us. Collective spiritual practices like the corporate act of praying in public can shape protest space in profound ways. Inasmuch as the work of antiracism is going to at least at some points result in public protest, this lesson is essential to remember. Even though bringing a collective practice like public prayer to bear on the racism of society does not forestall the possibility of violent reprisal—and in fact some research suggests that, at least in the case of the mid-twentieth-century Black freedom struggle, praying in public as part of a protest could actually invite violence in return—it does ground the action, center it, give it a gravitas and integrity that individual actions, no matter how well intentioned or religiously adorned, simply cannot offer.

Collective action is powerful action. History makes this clear. It never happens by accident, however. Behind Birmingham, Danville, and McComb were organizers working to bring people to the table, identifying the timing of events, ensuring that there would be proper logistical support. The staff of SNCC and SCLC helped bring the stories we have described to fruition. And thus the related corollary: collective action is never accidental action. It is always intentional.

THE COLLECTIVE ROOTS OF OUR WORK—AND ITS LIMITS

When we first called members of the Anabaptist community together to address the topic of racism in our church community in early March 1995 at the Restoring Our Sight conference we described in the introduction, we did not do so just to have an event and be done with it. We made certain that the last session of the gathering would be a time of inviting people to think about, envision, and identify what would come next. After participants lifted up the possibility of groups working together to form teams focused on dismantling racism in their own institutions, we invested much of the next decade supporting them to do that very thing. It took careful planning, the investment of financial and human resources, and a whole lot of logistical coordination and relational fostering. It was hard and demanding work but also deeply fulfilling.

And it was always, always, collective.

A steering committee worked with us to plan and organize the Restoring Our Sight conference in Chicago. That group transitioned into the leadership committee that guided the Damascus Road process that followed. In our extended anti-racism process, we formed and molded teams, not individuals. We drew together a community of trainers and organizers. The two of us were—and remain—a team.

That collectivity does, however, come with challenges. Anyone who has ever joined a congregation, synagogue, mosque, temple, or sangha knows that being part of a group brings challenges as much as it does possibilities. Egos clash. Leaders fail. Families drift away. To invest one's self into a community, whether religious or civic, is to risk heartbreak and disappointment. Movements rise. Movements fall. Such is the reality of history.

In the late summer of 2017, Cheryl and Tobin were on vacation when White nationalists rallied in Charlottesville, Virginia. He picks up a story about their effort to respond to racism from a collective base:

Here I should note that both Cheryl and I identify as White people and the church I will reference was a predominantly White Presbyterian congregation in the Rocky Mountains.

When we returned from our time away, we asked a fellow member of our congregation whether anything had been said about the events during the previous Sunday's worship service. She said that there had been no mention of the events one way or another.

I was discouraged to hear this and got a little despondent.

It was at that point that Cheryl said, "Well, we are part of this worshiping community. We can invite our community to respond." So after discussing it with an interracial couple at our congregation, we together crafted a statement. This is what it said:

> The White supremacy rally in Charlottesville, Virginia, on Saturday, August 12, 2017, revealed a disturbing level of hatred, animosity, and racist rhetoric, much of it directed toward clergy members present in nonviolent witness. As members of a Christian church community in the state with the highest concentration of hate groups per capita in the country, we recognize our responsibility to bring our faith to bear in this present moment of increasing violence toward people of color and members of other faith communities.
>
> In the last year, members of our congregation have spent time learning about the Islamic community and the experience of Muslims in Montana. We have also sponsored adult Sunday school classes on the history and present practice of racism in our state and city. Those conversations have left us ever more aware of our own prejudices, of the threats faced on a regular basis by our Muslim sisters and brothers, and of our own history of separation and isolation from people who do not conform to the White, middle-class demographic that dominates our congregation. We have much to learn and much to confess.
>
> Yet we sense in this moment a new opportunity to raise our voices as Christians living out our faith in Missoula, Montana, and proclaim definitively that our congregation will be a place where all people are welcome. Race, nation, or religion will not bar anyone from our doors. As a community in which we are formed in our faith, one where we strive to grow in maturity as individuals and as a body of believers, we will also recommit ourselves to speaking up with both compassion and courage when we encounter racism and prejudice in our community, workplaces, and homes. We will not stay silent in the face of jokes, comments, or written communications that threaten, belittle, or

disparage anyone because of their race or religion. We will also support efforts in our city and state to oppose White supremacy organizations wherever they are active.

We pray that the voices raised in hatred and committed to White supremacy will abate. At the same time, we want to be part of preparing for a church community, city, state, and nation where all people are welcome and the vision of Revelation 7:9 is fully realized:

> After this I looked, and there was a great multitude that no one could count, from every nation, from all tribes and peoples and languages, standing before the throne and before the Lamb, robed in white, with palm branches in their hands.

In the recent past, we had served as elders and deacons in the congregation that we were inviting to support this statement. We had a strong relationship with the pastoral staff. So we sent the statement to our pastor—a White man—and asked if we could discuss it with the congregation's elders. After taking a few days to consider our request, he said he would not bring it to the elders. We pushed him on his decision and again asked him to at least allow discussion of the statement with the elders. He again refused. Instead, he proposed a service of confession open to the public in response to the events in Charlottesville.

We expressed how disappointed we were that he refused to bring the statement to the elders and requested a meeting with him, two elders—both White men—who had also been part of the conversation, the associate pastor—a White woman—and the interracial couple from the congregation who had partnered with us as we corresponded with the pastor.

During the subsequent meeting, we confronted the pastor and elders about how deeply betrayed we felt by their decision to not even allow the statement to be considered by the elders. When pressed, the pastor explained that he feared a backlash from conservative members of the congregation were they to even discuss the statement. He named two wealthy and influential members of the church in particular, both White men, as those he feared would respond negatively. By the end of the highly emotional and difficult meeting, the pastor confessed that he had acted out of fear and had acted inappropriately.

In the subsequent weeks, the pastor sought out and had one-on-one conversations with the four of us who had initiated and proposed the statement. He apologized and confessed what he felt was sinful behavior on his part. He asked for forgiveness. All of us reported having extended forgiveness but also were collectively disappointed that at no point did he initiate or allow for discussion of the statement from that point forward.

Within six months, the four of us who had drafted and initiated the statement left that congregation. We still have collegial relationships with members of the church and live just around the corner from the pastor and his family. Our decision to leave was a direct result of the fallout of these events but also arose from other factors, such as feeling exhausted from simultaneously addressing racism in multiple institutions. We realized we needed a worshiping community with whom we could connect and gain sustenance for the struggle rather than one that was the site of that struggle.

As this story suggests, collective action will not always succeed. Indeed, working to bring about corporate change may lead to separation and disjuncture if not outright setback. There are no guarantees in this work. Nor do we get to know the ultimate ends of our efforts. Especially in the case of collective action. Corporate change is long-term and messy, and is realized only through focused, sustained, visionary action. It seems easier to focus just on changing ourselves and one or two people around us.

Those kinds of individual efforts are not unimportant, but they are ultimately ineffective if that is the limit of our focus. In a recent antiracism session, a White male participant working for a Mennonite institution pushed back against our choice to focus on institutional transformation. He declared, "Changing hearts and minds, that's what will make the difference. Changing institutions has failed." The response we offered in return was not to his liking: "All we can do is attest to our experience and the research we have done. Focusing on individual relationships alone simply does not build a foundation to change systemic racism. We can do better than what we have been taught thus far. We invite you to join us in that effort."

Whether that specific individual will eventually join efforts to transform the very organization for which he works remains to be seen. But history reminds us again and again of the power of collective action, of focusing on changing how employees are held accountable at their jobs, of transforming what those staff responsibilities themselves entail, of equipping the institutions to address and weather the backlash that almost always emerges amid naming and working to dismantle racism where it occurs.

And collective action can lead to transformation. It does not always result in discouragement and dissolution. A story that Tobin tells from Community Mennonite Church in Markham, Illinois, makes that evident.[3]

COMMUNITY MENNONITE'S INTERRACIAL CHRISTMAS

The Christmas pageant at Community Mennonite Church was always a treat. The brick walls festooned with greenery. The eager anticipation of young children bursting into chatter and antics and no small bit of mayhem. Christmas carols. Advent wreaths. Food and friends and beauty. For the six years we worshiped with that congregation between 2002 and 2008, I don't think we ever missed a pageant.

One of those years Cheryl played the part of Mary. A young man from the youth group played Joseph. Another year, I played Joseph, and the wife of one of our pastors played Mary. In both instances, as was the case most every year, the holy couple was interracial.

Not such a big deal, that. Not in 2021. Although commercials featuring interracial couples still ignite the ire of White supremacists and interracial couples report instances of social ostracism and harassment, interracial marriages have grown more commonplace and socially acceptable—at least as compared to 1963.

I mention 1963 because that was the year when the depiction of an interracial holy couple in Community Mennonite's Christmas pageant did cause a hullabaloo. A big one. They had to call in the denominational heavyweights. It was not, apparently, very pleasant.

This is how it went down.

By December 1963, Community had been experimenting with integration for a little over two years. One Sunday in 1961, three African American women attended a Sunday morning worship service at the previously all-White congregation. In 1956 when charter members had purchased property on which to construct a sanctuary, they had signed off on a restrictive covenant excluding "'any one who is not a Caucasian' from the premises." If ever there was an example of institutional racism made manifest, this was it. The congregation, nonetheless, welcomed the African American women.

Despite a few bumps along the way, a core of both White and Black members continued to attend. And by all accounts they enjoyed each other as they worshiped.

Yet tensions built below the surface. From the onset, some White members had raised concerns that an integrated congregation would lead, inevitably, to intermarriage. In keeping with the history of Black-White racial unions, the White community has been less supportive of interracial unions than the Black community has, a pattern especially true in the 1940s and '50s. Although White attitudes had begun to liberalize by the 1960s, the issue remained fraught in a community like Markham that was at that time in the midst of White flight. Black families had started to relocate to the community in search of a bit of suburban safety and security. Yet once again, systemic racism showed up.

In that context of rapidly changing racial demographics, a long history of White fear of interracial marriage, and a still fledgling congregation, the organizers of the 1963 Christmas pageant cast a Black Joseph and a White Mary. The service ensued. Christmas came and went. All apparently without incident.

Then the church board met on January 17. With the start of the new year came reports on attendance (it was up), heating of the church building (it had started), and offering envelopes (they should be numbered). Then the pastor at the time, Larry Voth, invited the field secretary for city churches from the national-level home Missions Commission of the General Conference Mennonite Church, Peter Ediger, to speak. Ediger noted that the rest of the denomination was very interested in what was happening in Markham as this small, formerly all-White congregation found itself on a journey toward racial integration. They were, indeed, embodying the kind of institutional transformation that so often seems elusive. He offered a word of encouragement by noting that when a congregation is "having a struggle for existance [*sic*] it is a living church."

All seemed in order.

And then it wasn't.

Church board chair Al Levreau read Genesis 11:1-9, the description of the Tower of Babel in which "the LORD confused the language of all the earth; and from there the LORD scattered them abroad over the face of all the earth." The notes from the meeting on January 17 don't explain what message Levreau meant to send by reading that passage. Perhaps he saw in the story of Babel's chaos a case study to be avoided as Community Mennonite embarked on racial integration.

What was clear was that he did not approve of mixed-race marriages. Not at all. Not even the hint of one in a Christmas play. With a generous dose of understatement bordering on cheekiness, the unidentified keeper of the minutes observed, "There was quite a discussion regarding inter-marriage."

It must have been *quite* a discussion. At the end of it Levreau had resigned from his position as board chair and declared that he would not return to worship services at CMC. After a unanimous vote to close the meeting, Ediger offered "a word of prayer."

I've often wondered what kind of conversations transpired in the church parking lot after this meeting. I imagine there was some venting. Perhaps even a bit of invective and opprobrium directed at the departing chairperson. A bit of self-righteous indignation even? Or there could as easily have been mourning and expressed concern for the sudden separation. After all, when the congregation had weathered a previous racial controversy, Levreau had been the one to lobby for an open-door policy that set the path toward the integrated nativity scene. The record doesn't say what the church leaders talked about as they prepared to go home.

A month later the board met again. This time the president of the entire General Conference joined the meeting on February 15. Although Levreau did not attend—and in fact had not been visited by church leadership since his abrupt departure—board member Margaret Carr also objected to the prospect of intermarriage and grilled conference executive Walter Gering on the denomination's position on the topic. After Carr explained her objections to both integration and intermarriage, Gering backpedaled by asserting that denominational officers had never encouraged intermarriage but that he thought Black and White couples could have a happy marriage. When prompted, African American board member William Smith explained that Black families in the congregation were not interested in marrying across racial lines, an assurance that Black church leaders had been stating to White Mennonites for nearly a decade.

The controversy came to an end a month later. A delegation reported that they had met with Levreau, but that he was not willing to return unless he could influence the church away from integration. Neither his heart nor his mind had, apparently, changed. Smith replied, "As well educated as we are, why do these things keep coming between us?" His incredulity at the prospect of a Christian brother objecting to his presence in the congregation leaps off the page across a half-century.

In response the board put their collective foot down. In short, they decided to change their institution. They voted—unanimously—to discontinue discussion about whether the church would be integrated and to declare—officially—that "Community Mennonite Church of Markham, Illinois[,] . . .

welcomes continued growth on a racially integrated basis." That decision itself changed not only the institution but the hearts and minds of many to come.

To be certain, changing institutions is demanding work. Seldom does it unfold without controversy. History could have gone in a different direction that night. Board members could have chosen to be silent, to allow the controversy to spill over into the congregation as a whole, or to simply decide that the bother wasn't worth it. Other majority White churches certainly did. But instead they set their faces toward an uncertain future and made the decision to continue trying to figure out what it would mean for Black people and White people to worship together.

I chose to write about this story because it is a Christmas story, and nativity narratives just don't get old. And also because I miss CMC's Christmas pageants. They were a fine thing. Always a bit chaotic around the edges. Sometimes the congregation's singing was a bit flat. It wasn't always entirely, well, polished. But the love in that room? That was unmistakable. And the holy couple—by tradition through the first decade of the twenty-first century, if not longer—was always interracial. The hope and promise of that image, however simplistic it may have been, never failed to move me.

I write this story on the morning of a day in which I will later denounce White nationalism at a local rally. Given the resurgence of White supremacy in our country, writing about an integrated Christmas service fifty years in the past can seem irrelevant if not naïve. To a degree, that may be true. But I also know that when I speak tonight, when I call out White nationalists for being small-minded, hard-fisted, and racist through and through, I will do so carrying a little bit of that nativity scene with me, and a little bit more of a congregation that decided to collectively say yes rather than no to the question of integration before them fifty years ago.

CONNECTING TO AN ANTIRACIST SPIRITUALITY: THE CONTAINERS

But what does any of this have to do with an antiracist spirituality? What difference does it make that we are discussing that spirituality in a collective rather than just an individual sense? First, we need to consider together how we both experience and shape an antiracist spirituality collectively, not just individually. In our final chapter we will discuss at greater length what the spiritual disciplines have to teach us—a focus that will attend to the individual aspects of those traditions and how they can shape our antiracist actions. Here, we want to touch on the corporate nature of that spirituality.

Three elements seem particularly important to explore. First is the container of that spirituality, the space that holds it and gives it form. Within the particular Christian tradition from which we come, that container has been the congregations of which we have been a part. Regina has already written about the formative, nurturing space that was Lee Heights in Cleveland. Tobin found a similarly racially integrated supportive community at Community Mennonite. Neither community was perfect, not by a long shot. But the congregational space that opened up amid whatever imperfections may have been at play far outweighed the human limitations. To return again to an idea we developed when discussing antiracism and popular culture, a profound, widespread, unabashed love permeated both congregations. Articulated on Sunday mornings from the pulpit, explored in small group and Sunday school discussions, made manifest in outreach and concrete in response to racism, the congregations created space each week for that love to invite growth, maturity, and courage among its members.

The congregations gave form and substance to the antiracist spirituality by offering a structure and a collective practice for its members. The physical buildings were important simply because they allowed people to come together in a space where they did not have to worry about racism showing up. Members' homes served a similar function. Again, they were not perfect, but those gatherings countered the segregation, homogeneity, and White supremacy of the society in which they were situated. And the weekly cycle of the events they hosted made certain that the members did not forget that they were loved, that they were intrinsically beloved, and that they could love in return despite the messages of the society around them which said otherwise.

One weekend, the two of us led a training workshop for Lee Heights members who were developing long-term plans for antiracist transformation in their local community. Partway through the training we paused the event, carpooled downtown, and participated in a local witness against corporate greed and racism. As we drove to the event, we talked together about the intersections between oppressions, their spiritual roots, and how resistance to oppression anywhere is resistance to oppression everywhere. It was no surprise to either of us that this kind of focused, grounded, and corporate practice—attending to both the long-term vision and the short-term practice—would emerge from this congregation. The Sunday after the public witness and the rest of the training, both events were named, celebrated, and lifted up in the course of Sunday worship. Because of personal circumstances, not everyone had been able to participate in the events, but they offered their support and encouragement when they gathered for worship.

The containers for collective antiracist growth and practice do not always take the form of a congregation. Synagogues, mosques, temples, and sanghas all serve similar purposes. But so do informal communities and circles of friends. Tobin and his wife Cheryl have for more than thirteen years been part of a weekly supper club that gathers for food and conversation. Although for most of its history that community has been made up of only White people, members of that supper club have talked about racism and its many manifestations on multiple occasions. Widerstand Consulting, the antiracism nonprofit that Cheryl and Tobin founded in the aftermath of the murder of George Floyd, owes its online delivery platform to connections made through that community. We have noticed that our children and their peers have formed similar support circles among friends and acquaintances and sometimes through political groups to which they belong. The point is not that a particular kind of group is better equipped than others to foster an antiracist spirituality. Rather, any space that invites individuals to join corporate reflection on their work and journey in the world and encourages action to push back against the racism present is a space where a collective antiracist spirituality can be and is regularly formed.

May more grow and develop.

CONNECTING TO AN ANTIRACIST SPIRITUALITY: THE CONTENT

The second area we would like to explore is the content of that container. We want to examine the stuff and content of that collective antiracist spirituality. We have observed several markers of that practice. Content—whether in the forms of prayers, songs, or reflections—that stems from and reflects back on a tradition offers powerful formative support. The more that communities of worship and resistance ground their collective spirituality in practices that bring a history to the room, the more present will be examples and meaning that offer sustenance for the long haul. This is the wisdom of the elders at work, the passing down of experience so that those who come after can gain from those who have gone before.

Communities that draw their members' attention to bring their spiritual resources to brokenness and despair rather than point them away from it likewise have much more effective track records in preparing their members for the difficult work of dismantling racism. This raises the issue of theodicy, a ten-dollar theological word which asks how we reconcile the prospect of an all-powerful, all-good God with the very real and recurrent reality of evil in the world. How could such a God allow such things to unfold?

In the White Western theological tradition, theologians have come up with a number of ways of addressing this problem: God is mystery; God's plans are unknowable; creation is not finished; free will; among others.

Instead of exploring those ideas, we want to draw attention to how church leaders and theologians in the Black theological tradition have responded to this issue. In short, they have said it simply: It isn't worth our time to bother about it.

We know that evil happens, they assert. As descendants of enslaved Africans who face the largely unmitigated effects of systemic racism today, that evil is ongoing.

But what has that to do with the way God acts in the world? In the main, the Black theological tradition asserts instead that this world is a broken place and that in the midst of that brokenness, our energy is better spent acting as God's representatives in it. Is that not a better use of our time and energy than trying to solve a theological puzzle that even if solved may not make a difference in how we respond to the presence of evil?

The Black theological tradition offers that profound gift, a fundamental theological insight. Be about the business of overcoming evil. Let go of the desire to figure out why that evil exists. Some even suggest that the reason these White, Western scholars have the time and energy to prioritize such questions is because of their privilege.

So when a White driver of a blue pickup plowed into a row of African American protestors kneeling and praying outside a segregated swimming pool in Cairo, Illinois, in 1962 and struck down a thirteen-year-old girl—the only one who refused to move as the driver approached—the question was not, How could God let something like that happen? The question was, What are we going to do now? The answer for the civil rights workers in the area was, We will continue. We will not stop.

This is the content of an antiracist spirituality in action, a pointing of its members to the hurt of the world and a response to it with courage and good focus. Once again, the collective practice of a spiritual tradition led to collective action.

One additional marker of the content of an antiracist spirituality deserves brief mention. That is its tone and tenor. We often find ourselves struck by how White religious communities of which we have been a part are very uncomfortable with expressions of anger at injustice. To be certain, the expression of anger—especially by White men—frequently shuts down deeper reflection and collaboration. It can also be abusive. Political discourse in the twenty-first century has too often been defined by anger and invective. Yet an authentic and robust antiracist spirituality needs also to make room for an anger at the injustice of racism that does not shut down others or prove abusive. Martin Luther King Jr.'s sermons show flashes of this kind of anger. So, too, the public oratory of Fannie Lou Hamer. An antiracist spirituality of the kind we have observed to be most effective makes room for the full breadth of human emotion but is always grounded in and returns to an unmitigated and unrelenting love of self, of community, and of adversary.

CONNECTING TO AN ANTIRACIST SPIRITUALITY: THE CONSUMPTION

Container. Content.

And then there is consumption.

This is not the consumption of consumer goods. It is not the indulgence to excess of that which is unhealthy. Rather, this third marker of a collective antiracist spirituality is the consumption of the content of that spirituality and making it our own. This is the difference the practice of corporate prayer makes as we go about the business of our daily lives. It is the internalizing of how one chooses to respond to an instance of racism in a business meeting, at a family gathering, in the middle of a sales pitch. The consumption of an antiracist spirituality results in the fortitude and energy to form a community of resistance and together make a choice to make a difference in the groups from which you come.

In this sense the consumption of those antiracist spiritual resources is a holy act. It is made possible only through the form and support of a collective gathered together and supportive of each other; this is where the language and vocabulary of the rituals and rites of communion in the Christian tradition help shape our understanding of what the consumption of an antiracist spirituality ultimately means. We share together in the memory of an act of violence. We recognize that a community grieved a profound and unutterable loss. Through symbol and sharing, we raise the promise of a wholeness restored against all odds. Despite hope abandoned. Renewal awaits.

This is the promise that a collective antiracist spirituality ultimately holds up. Regardless of our particular spiritual tradition, a practice that invites individuals to be present with each other, sustains them on a regular basis, offers the hope of history, and fosters the enactment of that resistance in one's daily being is what can make a difference.

In the end, we assert, it is the only thing that ever has.

Chapter 10

Antiracism and Spiritual Discipline

We write this chapter with caution. In our work with groups, until now we have consciously avoided spiritualizing antiracism because of wariness around unintended results of false piety ("what a good antiracist I am") or a "once and done, I've repented for my sins and the sins of my ancestors, now leave me alone" attitude. Even so, we recognize the necessity of the language and practice of spirituality in our antiracism work. We also recognize that not everyone engaged in antiracism work is religious. In either case, we think these musings will be useful.

The work of antiracism has at least three broad components: bearing witness, fostering justice, and sustaining work for the long haul. These components are active and are best done in community. This is what has sustained our work over the long haul, particularly through difficult times. They are practices, and for us as people of faith, spiritual disciplines.

Bearing witness happens when we face the truth of our history, understand how it has brought us to the present moment, and also face the atrocities that continue to occur as part of ongoing systemic racism. Working for justice involves interrupting systems of oppression and working for healing of those who have been and continue to be harmed. All of this work requires resilience.

If it seems strange to think of doing the work of antiracism through the practice of spiritual disciplines, perhaps it will help to examine how racism (as well as other systemic forms of oppression) operates as a set of sanctioned, embodied practices that form a culture strong enough that after a while, most people don't even question it—it's "just the way things are."

Structural violence begins with dehumanization. After the period of enslavement, it took the continued systemic denial of Black people's humanity to convince people that African Americans needed to be segregated from White society in all ways possible. This practice of dehumanization and subsequent segregation took on the form of ritualized behavior—a sequence of activities performed over and over for a particular purpose. Rituals are a sign of belief and a way of honoring one's religious code. They are a form of responsibility, performing an act at a specific time and in specific ways.

For most of the history of the United States, segregation has determined place for people. Entire cities are mapped onto racialized geographies put in place by tradition and legislation and still held in place by continued practice. These practices were highly ritualized to firmly entrench the idea that Black bodies should be kept apart and away from White people.

In the 1950s, Ruth Eigsti, a Goshen College sociology student, wrote her senior thesis about the fears of the White community in Goshen over the possibility of Black people moving into town.[1] She primarily interviewed business owners, asking if they would hire a Black person, and what their thoughts were about Black people moving into town. Their responses expressed anxiety about upsetting the common practice of racial segregation. They gave answers in keeping with justification of segregation across the United States: safety, property values, and fear of what others might think or do. White people had been socialized to believe certain stereotypes about Black people (even though they didn't know any, or knew very few) and that ending segregation would be to upset the order of things. Eigsti writes,

> The reason people would hesitate to accept the Negro is due to the different standards they have, compared to the whites. The Jews have been accepted because they measure up to the standards of the people in town. He would not discriminate in hiring because of color and does not think his workers would care. People in this city are not thinking about this problem because most of them have never been confronted with it. When asked his personal opinion he replied the property would be lowered. A high class would be all right (sic) but the ones always moving around are not usually of that type.
>
> Another said, reflecting his personal opinion, if Negroes would be cleaner, and take more pride in their homes, they would not be stereotyped as much as they are. He recognizes that conditions in East Goshen are as deplorable as some Negro sections, but the influx of Negroes would not help. Property value goes down as Negroes move in and take over. He believes more education for the Negro would correct many of the social evils that are attached to them. A Negro family from New Paris goes to his church. Puerto Ricans are accepted in his factory as well as D.P.'s from Central Europe. He does not hold that all Negroes are of the lowest class. He concludes that they make good servants.[2]

Segregation became ritualized in ways that defied common sense, but still it persisted. To keep Black patrons separate, businesses would of course refuse service. To avoid missing out on sales, many opted to provide service but away from the eyes of White customers. So Black people could not eat in a restaurant, but they could order, pay for, and receive food (and other goods) through the back door or a side window. Nightclubs and other entertainment venues would hire Black talent but would not allow their Black relatives and friends to come and enjoy the show. Or, in the case of Marian Anderson and the Daughters of the American Revolution, a singer would be invited to sing but denied entry into the very hall to which she was invited.

A specific kind of ritual was also embedded in the functioning of segregated public transportation systems in many parts of the country. Many are familiar with the Montgomery bus boycott of 1955–56, especially the mythologized version that casts Rosa Parks as a mere tired seamstress who one fine day stood her ground, and then the civil rights movement sprang fully formed from the seat she refused to give up on that bus. (The real story is much more complicated, and more interesting, and demonstrates the power of solidarity and coalition.)

In Montgomery, the front half of the bus was reserved for White riders, the back for African Americans. However, if all the seats in the front of the bus, in the White section, were full, it was incumbent upon Black riders to give up their seats for White riders. In addition to keeping the races separate, the bus ritual served as a daily reminder for its riders, the citizens of Montgomery, of the racial hierarchy in operation. The buses had two doors: one in the front and one in the back. Some drivers would require their Black passengers to enter the front of the bus to pay their fare, get off the bus, and walk around to the back and enter through the rear door. The message was clear as bus riders daily embodied their status as "back of the bus."

The way that Parks's story has traditionally been told—"Parks was a tired African American seamstress who one day refused to give up her seat on a bus in Montgomery, Alabama, to a White man, and by doing so, she bravely, accidently, and singlehandedly launched the civil rights movement which eventually prevailed"—lifts Parks up and out of her community and her history. In fact, Rosa McCauley Parks was a well-read, conscious activist who came from a family of activists. Her own definition of herself was as a rebellious person. The circumstances around her helped shape this sense of rebelliousness.

Born in 1913, she was the grandchild of enslaved people; her grandfather was the slave owner's son. The women in her family in particular—her mother and her grandmother—raised her to not think of herself as inferior to any person. As a child, she witnessed the escalation of Klan violence after World War I. She would have been six years old during what was called the Red Summer of 1919 when Black soldiers returned from war, expecting that they had now earned the right to be treated as equal Americans. In her town, churches were burned and Black people were whipped and killed, found dead in the streets.

Parks was an early and avid reader, and was raised on the notion that a primary goal of education was learning and claiming the history of Black resistance. Her consciousness developed not only from events happening in the world but from how her family talked about it.

At home, the McCauleys discussed the history of slavery, the situation of blacks in Alabama, and how "to survive, not getting into trouble by confrontation with white people who were not friendly to us." Rosa's family sought to teach her a controlled anger, a survival strategy that balanced compliance and militancy. One of the lessons [her mother] imparted that lodged in Rosa's head was how "slaves had to fool the white people into thinking that they were happy. The white people would get angry if the slaves acted unhappy. They would also treat the slaves better if they thought the slaves liked white people." As she became aware of the terms of white supremacy, the fact that acting happy produced better treatment stuck in her throat. She longed for ways to contest this treatment. She also well understood the punishment for resistance.[3]

Parks would constantly have to battle these two forces: militancy could get a person killed, and yet resistance, however dangerous, pushed back on the oppression and at times made it diminish.

In the summer of 1955, when she was forty-two years old, Parks spent two weeks at the Highlander Folk School in Tennessee. The Highlander school was a place for Black and White activists to train, to plan. At this point, Parks had been an organizer for years, but was discouraged by what seemed like little to no change. For two weeks at the center, she worked at plans for desegregating schools, but didn't have much hope for any kind of change in Montgomery.

But on December 1, 1955, Parks refused to give up her seat for a White man, the third African American woman within a year to do so. Like the other women before her, she was arrested. The next day, the Women's Political Council, which had been strategizing for over a year about the buses, called for a one-day boycott. As people began to mobilize, the twenty-six-year-old pastor of Dexter Avenue Baptist Church, Martin King, was elected as the president of the newly formed Montgomery Improvement Association.

The bus boycott lasted for 381 days. It was a win, with a federal district court eventually declaring segregation unconstitutional and the Supreme Court upholding the decision.

Ironically, by the time the mass meetings were organizing, Parks's voice was diminished. Many of the participants of the civil rights movement have acknowledged that much of the visible leadership, including those whose voices were heard at the gatherings and those who spoke for the movement, was often male. But women were there. And young people were there. Ordinary people, scores of ordinary people, made the bus boycott a success. And this is the genius of movements; they are made of people. There is no lone superstar that singlehandedly pulled this campaign off.

We tell the story of Rosa Parks here in this chapter on antiracism and spiritual disciplines because her example reminds us of the insidiousness of the systems against which we struggle and the courage it takes to bear witness to it.

Nothing more.

And certainly nothing less.

In this book, we have sought to make a case for choosing antiracism practices as a way of life and as a way of being in solidarity and community with others. We have learned that it is work that takes a lifetime. When I (Regina) was first engaged with what I then called "diversity work," I really believed that things would be different once my young children were adults. I have the same hopes that I did thirty years ago, but now I know more about the insidiousness and self-preserving and self-perpetuating power of racism.

More and more, we are coming to realize that the notion of White supremacy exerts seductive power and that racism reinvents itself over and over again, generation after generation, refreshing and renewing itself to fit in with the times.

Technological advances that we thought would bring the world together have also served to assist tribalism and echo chambers and stoke fears among White people who recognize that in a racist, capitalist society, one of the things that gives some measure of power is Whiteness. Things have changed: the end of legalized segregation, increases in media representation, and yes, even the first Black president. But we were mistaken in thinking that once those hurdles were overcome, the road ahead would be easier.

The first decades of the twenty-first century have been distressing, particularly concerning the heightened visibility of police brutality (for it is not new), but also the disparity in quality of life evidenced by the persistence of infant mortality, environmental racism, the school-to-prison pipeline, mass incarceration, and so much more. From that perspective, it's easy to believe that no progress has been made at all. Because we remind people of this, we are sometimes criticized for dwelling on all that is not yet done, instead of celebrating the achievements.

We do believe change is possible—we have seen and experienced it. But if we may say so, we have also become seasoned enough to recognize that we must keep our foot on the gas. Generations of Black people lived in this nation before being allowed to be citizens, to own property, to vote, to move into any neighborhood we could afford and send our children to school without fear of them being attacked. If it took hundreds of years to get to that point, we know it will take more than fifty or sixty to approach real equity for Black people and other People of Color.

A key component of the discipline we bring to the work of antiracism is coalition building and the networking required to make it effective. It is the primary means through which we are engaged in the second arena of antiracism spiritual disciplines—fostering justice.

I (Regina) don't need White people to befriend me so that they can become pleasantly astonished at how human I am and then not mind being around me, living near me, being supervised or taught by me when the world has conditioned them to suspect me, fear me, assume I have no intellect and that I will bring your property values down, lower your workplace standards, and so on. While all of those outcomes are lovely (and even desirable if we are going to be friends), they are not what I need. What I need from White people is to assume that I am human and because of that to want to work on behalf of my humanity just as you want others to work on behalf of yours. We need coalitions.

In 1981, Bernice Johnson Reagon, founder of the women's a capella singing group Sweet Honey in the Rock, gave an address called "Coalition Politics: Turning of the Century" at the West Coast Women's Music Festival in Yosemite National Forest. In the address, she identified the difficulty of breathing for those who were not acclimated to the environment, contrasted with those who were born in high altitudes and were breathing just fine: "You got one group of people who are in a strain—and the group of people who are feeling fine are trying to figure out why you're staggering around." This is what coalition work can feel like, she explained.

> I believe that we are positioned to have the opportunity to have something to do with what makes it into the next century. And the principles of coalition are directly related to that. You don't go into coalition because you just like it. The only reason you would consider trying to team up with somebody who could possibly kill you, is because that's the only way you can figure you can stay alive. . . .

We've pretty much come to the end of a time when you can have a space that is "yours only"—just for the people you want to be there. Even when we have our "women-only" festivals, there is no such thing. The fault is not necessarily with the organizers of the gathering. To a large extent it's because we have just finished with that kind of isolating. There is no hiding place. There is nowhere you can go and only be with people who are like you. It's over. Give it up.[4]

Coalition building, Reagon went on to say, means not remaining comfortable in little barred rooms where we have carried all our stuff and everyone looks like us and we're comfortable. Because then we realize we don't want to seem exclusive, so we open the door and let some folks in—the right kind of folks. But then other folks will come knocking on the door, and the next thing that happens is the room doesn't feel like the room anymore. And it isn't, because coalition building does not happen in a barred-off room.

Coalition building is one of the best expressions of an idea embedded in many religious systems—that one should treat others the way one wants (or expects) to be treated.

For Christians, of course, this is expressed in Jesus' response to the lawyer—quoting the Torah, Jesus says our first obligation is to love the One who created us (and demonstrate that love by loving creation) and to love our neighbor, who it turns out does not have to be the one who is just like me. To love each other is not about squishy feelings and general regard. It is caring for the life and welfare of those we share the planet with; it is making sure that obstacles to each other's well-being are removed. That is a big work.

We need coalitions because there is more work to be done than any of us can do on our own. If we make decisions only by majority-rule voting, we have a system made up of winners and losers. Coalition building builds in more awareness of our differences, our different abilities and needs. Coalitions make all of us stronger. Very practically, for Black people in the United States, we need others to join in our struggle because we are still only 13 percent of the population.

Even though in this book we have focused on the Black experience with racism, we know that if we are not aware of and engaged in the antiracist work on behalf of other People of Color, our work does not have integrity. It is our responsibility, at the very least, to know how our community and our actions contribute to the oppression of other People of Color. And we want to do more than the very least. We don't always get it right. We don't always show up. We need the disciplines for ourselves. We don't know everything about everything, and that's okay because we can depend on (and learn from) other people's knowing. Practicing awareness and bearing witness are places to start.

Recognizing that people are at different places in their journeys can help in our strategizing. It's tempting to scoff at or shame people who reject the truth about the history of this country's racism. Shame is a poor motivator of change, and our teaching and organizing cannot be shame-based. We cannot build strong coalitions by shaming people. However, we can make a distinction between shaming people and uncovering the truth and dealing with what has happened in the past. The reactions to teaching critical race theory in this country rely on making people think that acknowledging the violent racist past of the United States is meant to invoke shame. That is not the sole purpose. Yes, we should feel shame, but that shame should motivate us to dig up all the vestiges of that past and not repeat the same mistakes. The presidential executive order establishing the 1776 Commission, meant to refute the 1619

Project, is such an exercise. The 1619 Project commemorated the four hundredth anniversary of the beginning of slavery in the Americas. The entire premise of the 1776 Commission was built on the idea that we should never feel shame, only pride, in our country and we should not even mention, let alone dwell on, the parts where we didn't get it right.

We don't knock friendship or relationship building as a path toward an antiracist future. But we also know that by itself this has not worked, because those friendships and relationships often fall apart when the unequal power imbalance comes into play. Trust immediately breaks down when White supremacy is chosen over justice and equality. It happens in myriad ways in the workplace, in neighborhoods and schools, and at church.

Over the years we have seen many iterations and practices of working against racism. While we have evolved in our personal work and our work together, for thirty years we have tried to stay true to what we believe is crucial to doing work that is both transformative and sustainable and honors the humanity of those engaged in doing the work. We have made mistakes, and they have been humbling. They range from the ridiculous—like when we had a whole session built around a segment of a Disney video that Regina left in the family DVR at home, so we had to come up with a new idea on the fly. Some mistakes were more serious and for those we still have regrets, like when we backed down from aligning ourselves with those who were naming the structural violence of heterosexism in the church.

Not everyone agrees with how we do our work. Some people believe Black people should not invest any more energy in doing antiracism work with White people; this has meant folks have mistrusted Regina for working in predominantly

White institutions, doing antiracism work with White people, and being in an interracial relationship. Tobin has encountered death threats after he was put on a White nationalist–adjacent "professor watchlist" for speaking about systemic racism in public, he and his wife had to leave a worshiping community because of that church's refusal to speak out publicly against racism, and in more instances than he can remember he has been accused of being a "problem" because he brought up the issue of racism without apology. We both have found that some folks simply don't want to talk about power (this seems especially true for Protestant Christians).

Neither of us are surprised when these things happen.

Yet we are disappointed.

Here is what seems to be true: people resonate with the language we use to explain the purpose and function of racism—to uphold White supremacy despite the best efforts of people to overcome it. We have tried something called "racial reconciliation" without acknowledging that it's impossible to reconcile what has never been united. We have not had a period of time when people of different races have experienced societal equality on a structural scale. As we have noted and experienced, there is power in people's friendships and relationships across racial lines. The problem is, we have been told (by racial reconcilers) that relationships will be what changes the dynamics of racism. Clearly this is not true; while there are more and more interracial marriages and transracial adoptions than ever, structural and systemic racism still exists.

So if relational solutions don't work, what does? At the core of the spiritual discipline we are here promoting is the work of building a sustainable movement, the third primary spiritual discipline we promote.

Poet, essayist, and activist Audre Lorde wrote a series of essays about her battle with the cancer that eventually ended her life. In addition to the illness, Lorde also struggled to pay medical expenses and to continue her work as an educator and activist within institutions that seemed to be working to silence her. Of these struggles in the midst of her illness, she wrote, "Caring for myself is not self-indulgence, it is self-preservation, and that is an act of political warfare."[5] Those who would commit themselves to the work of healing must be equipped to tend to their own wounds. We must commit ourselves to radical acts of self-care. Self-care is part of the foundation for doing social justice work; if we are not working on our own wholeness (shalom), then it will be that much harder to work for wholeness on behalf of other individuals or systems. Recognition of and tending to our own humanity is critical. Structures of violence and injustice operate by dehumanizing, therefore a first step in undoing cycles of violence is recognizing patterns of dehumanization and interrupting them.

We don't revisit the stories we have shared in this book to rest upon days gone by, in the same way that we don't abandon our faith narratives after we have heard them once. We tell these stories, the real, complicated human versions of them, to celebrate them, yes. But also to equip us for the now. The threats of racism, poverty, and war are still with us. The work is not done. The work of liberation is not done in isolation. It is not done absent of community. It does not happen without being informed, or without the realization of how oppressions are connected.

In the spring of 2017, we both spoke at a reunion of the Minority Ministries Council held in Goshen, Indiana. During the late 1960s and early 1970s, members of the MMC had named the racism of the Mennonite Church. They did so in uncompromising ways that included not only calling out specific racist practices of Mennonite leaders and institutions but also challenging the church to invest significant financial resources in supporting leadership and congregational development of Black, Latinx, and Native American communities. The conference included a celebration of the witness of MMC leaders—many of whom had left or been forced out of the church for their antiracist actions—and an opportunity for students from Goshen College to conduct oral history interviews with dozens of those leaders.

Two moments capture the antiracist spiritual discipline that we have explored in this chapter. The first came at the end of the conference when the executive director of Mennonite Central Committee Central States, Michelle Armster, led a "ritual of blessing" for "a new generation of leaders." Regina's son Joshua Stoltzfus, who reported on the event for the national church press, wrote that "Armster called all attendees age 35 and younger to come forward and MMC leaders took turns handing them a candle or a stone, as a symbol of passing on a blessing for leadership to a new generation."[6] It was a powerful moment, one made all the more powerful in the reporting that followed because Regina had given birth to Josh the year that we co-founded the Damascus Road antiracism process. Many of the young people being blessed had participated in that training and it had informed their activism in the church.

This was a holy moment not only of honoring those who had long borne witness, who had fostered justice, and who had been in the work for the long haul but also of preparing the way for the next generation to do the same.

A holy moment, indeed.

The second came a bit earlier. This photo captures it.

Regina is on the left pointing at our friend and colleague Dr. Felipe Hinojosa, another longtime co-struggler in this work. Tobin, on the right, has his hand on Felipe's shoulder while Dr. Gilberto Pérez of Goshen College looks on. It was a moment of levity. Not at all rare in our work together. We were teasing Felipe about—something. None of us can remember exactly what. That's also telling. We tease each other a lot. This moment was in no way special.

And yet it was.

Because that moment of laughter and human connection was a result of the work we had done together in bearing witness to racism even when it was difficult, in fostering justice amid systems that had done all they could to silence our message, and in staying at it, not running away, getting up and doing the work again. The struggle and the laughter—they are always connected.

Later on that same day the leaders of the MMC called the two of us to the front of the room where we had just finished eating dinner. They presented each of us with a mug and honored us for the work we have done together.

We laughed—and cried—then too.

Conclusion

A Conversation We Had about the Book We Had Just Written Which Sums It Up—and Then Some—with a Coda

*S*o, *Regina, lets figure out what to do with this conclusion.*
Why are you pointing at me, Tobin?

Because it's your turn now. We're going to go back and forth. I'm thinking this could be a cool way to finish the book. You know—with a conversation about the book that we have just written.

Okay, okay. So we're going to talk about the conclusion.

Right. I'll be speaking in italics. You'll be speaking in non-italics. So our readers can keep track of who is saying what.

I want to loop back to what it has meant to still be in a close friend relationship and also a working relationship across racial lines after all of these years. That is something that a lot of people don't seem to do well, or they instead compartmentalize conversations about racism so that the friendship remains.

Friendship does seem to be the place to start. We wanted to have a closing story that would capture the themes we have explored in this book. We could have referenced any number of the institutions we worked with, but none of them seemed to capture the full complexity of what we have been writing about. So instead, here we are talking with each other as we ask the question, "What was it like to write this book?"

Yes. I think the first thing to note is that we wrote this book from the places we are now, which are very different from where we each were thirty years ago—both geographically and professionally. I think it is interesting that out of that group of core trainers who we brought together, so many of us ended up in academia. Calenthia [Dowdy] was already in academia.

Felipe [Hinojosa] did. You did. I did. Michelle [Armster] is now working on her doctorate as well.

I think both of us recognized that we would be doing antiracism work for the long haul, and we needed to figure out how to make that happen. So we came to the conclusion, "This is a thing that I am going to be doing the rest of my life. I don't know what it'll look like, but this is something that I am that has grabbed ahold of me. I can't just stop and say, 'I can quit you, antiracism.'"

I feel very fortunate that I'm able to do this work as a big part of my day-to-day teaching job. I get paid for it. And we both ended up as professors with different but similar situations.

I'm remembering, Regina, a conversation we had at the point where we were both preparing for or had already announced our departures from our Damascus Road leadership roles. We talked about founding an antiracism institute at some point in the future.

[Inhales.] Yes!

And, maybe we're there right now. We're not there yet in full but we're also sorta there already.

Yeah, yeah, yeah.

With Widerstand and Roots of Justice and this book—and how that all comes together, it feels like what we are doing now is in keeping with the vision for that antiracism institute.

I don't think we could have arrived at this point of pursuing an antiracist spirituality and doing this formal work together without—at least in terms of my part of the equation—having done some very intentional work around the spiritual disciplines.

There were things that I as a White man had to address in terms of my ego. It's ongoing. I'll be working on those issues for the rest of my life. But I also can say with confidence that I am at this point a better training and consulting partner with you and other People of Color than when I started.

I think a lot of that growth has come from recognizing the SMALLNESS of my role and also the SIGNIFICANCE of my role and coming to terms with both. That would not have been possible without the spiritual disciplines that we discussed in the last chapter.

Similarly to what you just expressed, my discernment process a few years ago led me to this central question—"What work am I going to say yes to?" I have choices about it. And because I am committed to continuing to do this work at a sustainable pace, I also had to make some choices about where I could not be, where I could not stay, what I could not do.

In that vein I'm thinking about the gaps. Ever since we met, there's never been a time when we did not know where each other was or how to get in touch. Those were times when I said to myself, "Okay, you're raising those kids and going to graduate school and all that kind of stuff and I'm over here." So there's something about that time apart.

What is it I'm trying to say?

I don't know if this is what you're trying to say, but what I was thinking earlier is that our work together has been made possible as much by the space apart as the space in connection. It is similar to the way that the process of caucusing makes us stronger. I think there's some parallel here. You've done some work with other women of color and with People of Color more generally. I've done work with White folks, with White men in other settings, and that's allowed us to come back together in more productive and healthy ways.

And part of that is choosing where we're going to do the work and with whom we are going to do the work. But I think, too, a big part of an antiracist spirituality is asking, "What is going to give me life right now? And what is not going to give me life?" That is a really lucky and privileged place to be. I recognize that.

Even with the number of minor irritations that I have with higher ed politics, I still get to say what I want to say to my students and to my community. In the midst of that work I keep coming back to the question, "Where do I want to put my best energy? Where do I want to put energy for the sake of the work that I want to do in the world but also for the sake of balance and finding joy?"

You have spoken about the idea of breath and breathing as important to this work. Can you tell me what you mean by that? I find myself drawn to it. I'd like to hear more about what you mean. Is it a matter of centering?

So there are a number of places where it shows up in my own spiritual work. One is that every morning I do yoga. Every single morning. One of the reasons for doing so is because of the stupid groin injury I had last year. Every time I try to get back into running, I injure myself again. So I turned to yoga to prevent that.

I started out doing it just a few times a week and then I decided during quarantine—"You know, I've got time." And I've always liked to do any kind of workout first thing in the morning. But since last summer I made it more of a ritual. It's not a "get the yoga out of the way and get on with my day" sort of thing. Instead I listen to the instructors who are digitally with me and listen to them speak about the importance of being in your body and breathing.

So that's the yoga piece.

But there's also something that's very grounding for me within that practice which reminds me that I'm part of the created order. Our Christian origin story begins with breath, begins with God breathing into the human—the earth creature. In Hebrew, it is the *spirit* and *wind*. And in Greek, too, there's this connection between breath and life and wind. And then I think about all the stories we know about Black people whose lives have ended while they were saying, "I can't breathe."

So it's about being in a body and what that body means as part of the created order, as part of the system of racism. It's more than skin color, but that's what people know. They know that race has something to do with skin color somewhere and that it's one of the ways that we as a human family are divided.

I think that on the surface I'm just struck by the parallels and the departures that come from thinking about the act of breathing. It's a part of our religious spiritual story. It's what happens when we are born. It's what leaves when we die.

That's really helpful and very profound. It makes me ask what the questions are for White people in this work especially given our collective predisposition to grab on to the universal before the particulars of race. We who are White would much rather talk about the humanity of it all, the universal application. We are much more uncomfortable talking about what a racial identity means for us as White people.

I was having a conversation with a number of other White antiracist organizers the week before last and one of our number was talking about the reality of historical trauma for White people. In particular, she explored the kind of trauma that comes from witnessing harm and genocide and colonialism and enslavement and not doing anything. These are such essential but also challenging topics because we also don't want to set up a parallel between historical trauma visited on the Indigenous, African American, Latinx, and Asian American communities and the kind of historical trauma that White people have encountered.

I continue to carry those concerns, but I do think that there's something in the concept of historical trauma for our spiritual exploration as White people. We need to ask ourselves, "What do we do with the legacy of having gone along with these horrors? How has that legacy affected our physical and emotional being?" We need to find ways to reconnect ourselves with everything that you've talked about—the breath, our spiritual traditions, the legacies of that acquiescence—but also the legacies of the witness and example of White people who have resisted racism.

This work of collective and individual reflection for White people continues to attract me. I want to try to find a way to do that reflection and exploration with integrity. I am hopeful that we who are White will eventually be able to acknowledge the need for us also to breathe and to remember that we are human but not superior. I am hopeful that we will be able to remember that our ways are A way. They are not THE way.

The shift is for us as White people to identify, fill, and define appropriate roles for ourselves in conversation with our colleagues of color. That's a matter of discernment and spiritual discipline and has much to do with the letting go of ego. It has much to do with accepting particular roles at particular times. But I think your metaphor of breath is helpful for that sense of centering, of being still, of setting aside ego.

At the same time I also don't want us to think that we can counsel away racism. I don't think that is possible. I don't think that a therapeutic approach is going to get rid of the problem, because we know that racism is a systemic reality and won't be undone by individual solutions. Yet the spiritual disciplines that we are talking about are a way to stay in the struggle to deal with that systemic dynamic.

Yes. And the staying in the struggle piece is one of the messages that I think is so essential. It's important for me. Because, you know, I used to quit after every training. In the early years that we worked together I was always declaring, "I'm out."

I remember this.

So in light of my repeated resignations, I eventually had to ask myself, "How do I make the time to make it possible for me to do this? What am I going to have to do more of? What am I going to have to do less of?" And, the *more of* is that interior work, especially after I've moved to northern Indiana. It is seeking out spaces where I can be with only People of Color, which has been hard during the COVID pandemic.

Having those spaces has been essential, but it has also been important to recognize that we might not ever get there. We probably won't. Wherever "there" is. But we have gotten to places where we can realize, "Oh, this place was like *this* and now it's like *this*." It had once been a place where the only People of Color who worked there worked in janitorial services. And now? Now this place is different.

Racism? Has it gone away? No. But there are some institutions that are better because they worked at undoing it.

All of this is to say, what I understand my work to be doing now is to have integrity about the way I walk around in the world. That's why I can't quit antiracism. Because I can't.

Do I fantasize about a day where I never have to think about racism? Yes. But is that day going to come? No. And that particular cost is challenging for many people—that you have to think about this every damn day, you have to at *least* think about it every day.

And if you think about it every day, and if you keep working at it and you learn more, you are going to apply that critical lens to stuff that used to bring you joy and now makes you irritating to your friends. Because now you can't watch a movie and be happy, because there's too much racism. That's peace studies all over the place.

My poor students. We get into the class like the one I'm teaching now on personal violence and healing where all we do for fifteen weeks is trauma, trauma, trauma, trauma, trauma. From racism to sexism to homophobia. But the other thing that's true about that class is, one week in, my students are saying to each other, "Oh, y'all are my people. My friends don't get why I study this or why I'm interested in talking about this."

And so I think that a big part of the work is building those kinds of places where we can look across the room and say, "Y'all are my people." Not because we're all the same, but because we are interested in making the world more like what it ought to be and so are making choices that make that future a reality.

I think we have a conclusion.

Do you?

I think that we are pretty darn close. I'm going to stop recording. Okay?

Okay.

A CODA

These are the final things that we want you to know about pursuing an antiracist spirituality.

That Tobin has long realized it is wise to trust Regina's instincts on just about everything.

That there are days when we don't know whether we are doing any good.

But that those are not all the days.

That the movement has its excesses and overstatements—like all movements have before.

But the elders bring wisdom. They ground us.

That antiracism work and the pursuit of a spirituality to sustain it has seasons. Stretches marked by desert expanse. Long weeks, months, even years, when there seems little progress and so much seems blocked.

And, also, moments and measures of time rich with laughter and the opening of ways.

We need to be ready to walk through both with equal acceptance.

That organizing is necessary.

But it sometimes forgets to be human and therefore can lose while winning.

That those of us who are White need to talk more about Whiteness and White supremacy and the systems that maintain it—we should never talk less about such topics, never less—but in so doing must never forget the belovedness that awaits us all.

That you can never listen too much.

That the way forward is sometimes to do nothing.

That struggle is part of the path.

But it should never become that which we seek.

That it is good to have friends who get you.

That there can come a point in one's life when the choices before you become more and more clear because a life lived with integrity points with less and less hesitancy to a certain horizon.

That to do the work of antiracism without pursuing a spirituality of the same is to invite an unmooring, to court a forgetting, to wander astray.

But to ground that work in that pursuit is to stand on a foundation, to look forward while remembering all that is true, and to step out with confidence holding a map in our hands.

Notes

CHAPTER 1

1. Rose Marie Berger, "'I've Known Rivers': The Story of Freedom Movement Leaders Rosemarie Freeney Harding and Vincent Harding," *Sojourners*, https://archive.li/KgCsJ.
2. Charles M. Payne, "Building Institutions, Teaching a Movement," in *Finding Mississippi in the National Civil Rights Narrative: Struggle, Institution Building, and Power at the Local Level* (Jackson: Fannie Lou Hamer National Institute on Citizenship and Democracy; National Endowment for the Humanities, 2014).
3. Michael Vinson Wiliams, "Medgar Evers," Mississippi Encyclopedia, last modified June 14, 2018, https://mississippiencyclopedia.org/entries/medgar-wiley-evers/.
4. Angelica Miller, "Wade, Andrew," Notable Kentucky African Americans Database, last modified December 10, 2020, https://nkaa.uky.edu/nkaa/items/show/300003773.
5. Sara M. Evans, *Personal Politics: The Roots of Women's Liberation in the Civil Rights Movement and the New Left*, 1st ed. (New York: Random House, 1979), 48.

6. Clayborne Carson, *In Struggle: SNCC and the Black Awakening of the 1960s* (Cambridge, MA: Harvard University Press, 1981), 206.

7. Anne Braden, "Finding the Other America," The November Coalition, accessed January 1, 2021, http://www.november.org/BottomsUp/reading/america.html.

8. Kyle Jantzen, "Research Report: Ben Goossen on Mennonites, Nazism, and the Holocaust," *Contemporary Church History Quarterly*, Volume 27, Number 1 (March 2021), https://contemporarychurchhistory.org/2021/03/research-report-ben-goossen-on-mennonites-nazism-and-the-holocaust/.

9. Iris de León-Hartshorn, "The Hard Work of Anti-Fascism: The Good, the Bad and the Ugly," MCC, June 22, 2020, https://mcc.org/centennial/100-stories/hard-work-anti-racism-good-bad-ugly.

CHAPTER 2

1. Judge Leon M. Bazile, "Indictment for Felony," court records, reproduction from microfilm, January 6, 1959, Caroline County (Va.) Commonwealth v. Richard Perry Loving and Mildred Dolores Jeter, 1958–1966, Caroline County (VA.) reel 79, Local Government Records Collection, Caroline County Court Records, Library of Virginia.

2. Katie G. Cannon, *Black Womanist Ethics*, American Academy of Religion Academy Series 60 (Atlanta: Scholars Press, 1988), 1.

3. Adelle M. Banks, "Despite Multiracial Congregation Boom, Some Black Congregants Report Prejudice," Religious News Service, April 28, 2021, https://religionnews.com/2021/04/28/despite-multiracial-congregation-boom-some-black-congregants-report-prejudice/.

4. Martí specifically uses the term *multiethnic* instead of *multiracial*.

5. Gerardo Martí, *A Mosaic of Believers: Diversity and Innovation in a Multiethnic Church* (Bloomington, IN: Indiana University Press, 2005).

6. Cannon, *Black Womanist Ethics*, 33.

CHAPTER 3

1. Scott Nakagawa, "Blackness Is the Fulcrum," *Race Files*, May 4, 2012, https://www.racefiles.com/2012/05/04/blackness-is-the-fulcrum/.

2. Ann Arnett Ferguson, *Bad Boys: Public Schools in the Making of Black Masculinity* (Ann Arbor: University of Michigan Press, 2000).

CHAPTER 4

1. Many thanks to Anthony Aiello, Tim Ballard, Amanda Barr, Jo Brown, Maren Haynes Marchesini, Susan Mark Landis, Hilary Jerome Scarsella, and Dylan Shearer for helping us identify and assess these examples.

CHAPTER 5

1. Christopher John Farley, "That Old Black Magic," *Time*, November 27, 2000, http://content.time.com/time/subscriber/article/0,33009,998604,00.html.
2. Portions of this discussion of the MAAF here and following first appeared as "Mennonites and the Magical African-American Friend," *Anabaptist Historians*, April 10, 2019, https://anabaptist historians.org/2019/04/10/mennonites-and-the-magical-african-american-friend/.
3. Linden M. Wenger and Virgil Brenneman, *Program of Witness to and with Negroes* (Chicago: Home Missions and Evangelism Committee Round Table, 1959), 1.
4. Wenger and Brenneman; William Pannell, "The Evangelical and Minority Groups," *Gospel Herald*, March 8, 1960, 205.
5. William E. Pannell, "Somewhere in the Middle," *Christian Living*, September 1968, 24.
6. William Pannell, "Little Black Sambo Still Lives," *The Mennonite*, February 16, 1971, 100.
7. John Powell, "AFRAM to Bring Blacks Together," *Gospel Herald*, July 31, 1973.
8. William E. Pannell, in-person interview by Robert Shuster, April 21, 1998, Billy Graham Center Archives, Wheaton College, Collection 498, Pannell, William E.; 1929-Interviews; 1995–2007, audio tapes, tape 3, available at https://ensemble.wheaton.edu/hapi/v1/contents/permalinks/Ne5q4L7G/view.
9. William E. Pannell, in-person interview by Robert Shuster, February 28, 2000, Billy Graham Center Archives, Wheaton College, Collection 498, Pannell, William E.; 1929-Interviews; 1995–2007,

audio tapes, tape 5, available at https://ensemble.wheaton.edu/
hapi/v1/contents/permalinks/Dz2e8FCa/view.

10. Pannell, interview, tape 5.

11. John S. Weber, "The History of Broad Street Mennonite Church
1936–1971" (senior thesis, Eastern Mennonite College, 1971), 46.

12. John E. Fretz, "Hard to Face It as It Is," *The Mennonite*, March 2,
1971, 150.

13. John Powell, for example, returned to the church, fulfilled a variety
of leadership roles, and continues to write a column for *Mennonite World Review*. James and Rowena Lark started a church in
Fresno, California, in the mid-1960s that did not have a Mennonite affiliation.

14. William Pannell, *My Friend, the Enemy* (Waco, TX: Word Books,
1968), 55.

CHAPTER 6

1. Portions of the discussion of White identity and spiritual formation
that follows first appeared as "And Then The Spirit Showed Up
(When I Really Didn't Want That to Be Happening): Whiteness
and Spiritual Formation," *Truth and Grace* (blog), December 17,
2020, http://tobinmillershearer.blogspot.com/2020/12/and-then-
spirit-showed-up-when-i-really.html.

2. W. E. Burghardt Du Bois, *Black Reconstruction in America: An
Essay toward a History of the Part Which Black Folk Played in the
Attempt to Reconstruct Democracy in America, 1860–1880* (New
York: Russell & Russell, 1935, 1963), 700.

3. The section that follows on White caucusing first appeared as
"The Discipline and Practice of White Caucusing," *Truth and
Grace* (blog), June 14, 2020, http://tobinmillershearer.blogspot
.com/2020/06/the-discipline-and-practice-of-white.html.

CHAPTER 7

1. "Nell Irvan [*sic*] Painter on Soul Murder and Slavery," PBS,
accessed July 13, 2016, http://www.pbs.org/wgbh/aia/part4/
4i3084.html.

2. "Painter on Soul Murder."

3. Nell Irwin Painter, *Soul Murder and Slavery*, The Fifteenth Annual
Charles Edmundson Historical Lectures (Waco, TX: Markham
Press Fund, Baylor University Press, 1995), 9.

4. Kelly M. Hoffmann, Sophie Trawalter, Jordan R. Axt, and M. Norman Oliver, "Racial Bias in Pain Assessment and Treatment Recommendations and False Beliefs about Biological Differences between Blacks and Whites," *Proceedings of the National Academy of Sciences of the United States of America* 113, no. 16 (April 19, 2016): 4296–301. https://doi.org/10.1073/pnas.1516047113.

5. Jamilia J. Blake and Rebecca Epstein, *Listening to Black Women and Girls: Lived Experience of Adultification Bias* (Washington, DC: Initiative on Gender, Justice and Opportunity, Georgetown Law, Center on Poverty and Inequality, 2019).

6. https://www.sentencingproject.org/criminal-justice-facts/.

7. Danielle Dirks and Jennifer C. Mueller, "Racism and Popular Culture," in *Handbook of the Sociology of Racial and Ethnic Relations*, ed. Hernán Vera and Joe R. Feagin (New York: Springer, 2007), 116, citing bell hooks, *Reel to Real: Race, Sex, and Class at the Movies* (New York: Routledge, 1996).

8. Gerardo Martí, *A Mosaic of Believers: Diversity and Innovation in a Multiethnic Church* (Bloomington: Indiana University Press, 2005).

9. Jacquelyn Grant, "Womanist Jesus and the Mutual Struggle for Liberation and on Containing God (Matthew 17:1-5 with Special Emphasis on Matthew 17:4)," *Journal for the Interdenominational Theological Center* 31 (September 1, 2003): 8.

10. J. H. O'Dell, "Life in Mississippi: An Interview with Fannie Lou Hamer," *Freedomways* 5 (1964): 235–36, quoted in Rosetta E. Ross, *Witnessing and Testifying: Black Women, Religion, and Civil Rights* (Minneapolis: Fortress Press, 2003), 113.

11. Fannie Lou Hamer, foreword to *Stranger at the Gates: A Summer in Mississippi*, ed. Tracy Sugarman (New York: Hill and Wang, 196), viii, quoted in Ross, *Witnessing and Testifying*, 114.

CHAPTER 9

1. Andrew Young, *An Easy Burden: The Civil Rights Movement and the Transformation of America* (New York: HarperCollins, 1996): 222–23.

2. Danny Lyon, *Memories of the Southern Civil Rights Movement* (Chapel Hill, NC: University of North Carolina Press, 1992), 63.

3. A version of the story about Community Mennonite that follows first appeared as Tobin Miller Shearer, "Christmas

Controversy: Community Mennonite, Interracial Marriage, and a Hope from a Half-Century Ago," *Anabaptist Historians*, December 21, 2018, https://anabaptisthistorians.org/2018/12/21/christmas-controversy-community-mennonite-interracial-marriage-and-a-hope-from-a-half-century-ago/.

CHAPTER 10

1. Ruth Eigsti, "Attitudes Representing Different Occupational Groups Toward the Negro in the City of Goshen" (senior thesis, Goshen College, April 1951).
2. Eigsti, 10.
3. Jeanne Theoharis, *The Rebellious Life of Mrs. Rosa Parks* (Boston: Beacon Press, 2013), 6.
4. B. J. Reagon, "Coalition Politics: Turning the Century," in *Home Girls: A Black Feminist Anthology*, ed. B. Smith (New York: Kitchen Table Press, 1983), 357.
5. Audre Lorde, *A Burst of Light: and Other Essays* (Mineola, MN: Ixia Press, 2017), 130. First published 1988.
6. Joshua Stoltzfus, "Minority Ministries Council Reconnects and Shares," *The Mennonite*, April 3, 2017, https://anabaptistworld.org/minority-ministries-council-reconnects-shares/.

The Authors

REGINA SHANDS STOLTZFUS

Regina Shands Stoltzfus was born in Cleveland, Ohio, and lived there for the first half of her life. She currently lives in Goshen, Indiana, and teaches at Goshen College in the Religion, Justice and Society department. Regina is co-founder of the Roots of Justice Anti-Oppression program (formerly Damascus Road Anti-Racism  Program) and has worked widely in peace education. She holds a master of arts degree in biblical studies from Ashland Theological Seminary and a PhD in theology and ethics from Chicago Theological Seminary. She is the author of two previous books, and her many articles have appeared in publications such as *Sojourners* and *The Mennonite*. She has also written for the *Anabaptist Historians* blog.

— TOBIN MILLER SHEARER →

TOBIN MILLER SHEARER

Tobin Miller Shearer is co-founder with Regina Shands Stoltzfus of the Damascus Road anti-racism process (now Roots of Justice) and an award-winning professor of history and African American studies at the University of Montana. He is the author or co-author of five books and more than one hundred articles. His work has appeared in publications such as the *Chicago Tribune*, *Conspire*, *The Mennonite*, and *Anabaptist Historians*. He blogs at *Truth and Grace*. Tobin is also the co-founder with Cheryl Miller Shearer of the anti-racism training and consulting nonprofit, Widerstand Consulting (www.WiderstandConsulting.org).

CPSIA information can be obtained
at www.ICGtesting.com
Printed in the USA
LVHW100753100123
736777LV00003B/550